VICTORY AT STALINGRAD

Also by Geoffrey Roberts

The Unholy Alliance: Stalin's Pact with Hitler

The Soviet Union and the Origins of the Second World War

The Soviet Union in World Politics, 1945–1991

Ireland and the Second World War (co-edited
with Brian Girvin)

The History and Narrative Reader (editor)

VICTORY AT STALINGRAD
THE BATTLE THAT CHANGED HISTORY

Geoffrey Roberts

An imprint of **Pearson Education**

London · New York · Toronto · Sydney · Tokyo · Singapore · Hong Kong · Cape Town
New Delhi · Madrid · Paris · Amsterdam · Munich · Milan · Stockholm

PEARSON EDUCATION LIMITED

Head Office:
Edinburgh Gate
Harlow CM20 2JE
Tel: +44 (0)1279 623623
Fax: +44 (0)1279 431059

London Office:
128 Long Acre
London WC2E 9AN
Tel: +44 (0)20 7447 2000
Fax: +44 (0)20 7447 2170
Website: www.history-minds.com

First published in Great Britain in 2002

ISBN 0 582 77185 4

British Library Cataloguing in Publication Data
A CIP catalog record for this book can be obtained from the British Library

Library of Congress Cataloging in Publication Data
A CIP catalog record for this book can be obtained from the Library of Congress

10 9 8 7 6 5 4 3 2 1

Typeset by Fakenham Photosetting Limited, Fakenham, Norfolk
Printed and bound in China.

The Publishers' policy is to use paper manufactured from sustainable forests.

CONTENTS

In Memory

of

Geoffrey Frank Weston, 1925–2001

PREFACE

The aims of this book are twofold. First, to provide an
overview of the battle of Stalingrad and its historical significance. Second, to summarise, synthesise and criticise the vast
literature on Stalingrad. No battle of any war has had more
written about it than Stalingrad. My main sources are indicated by citations in the text and in the guide to further reading at the end of the book. I have also drawn freely upon my
own specialist knowledge and expertise on wartime foreign
policy and diplomacy.

My interest in Stalingrad goes back to my childhood in
London in the 1950s and 1960s. I grew up in Deptford, in
south-east London – the most heavily-bombed area of
Britain. So there were plenty of bomb-sites, disused air raid
shelters, and concrete water tanks in which to re-fight the
battles of the Second World War. There were also lots of
family stories to fire the imagination. The block of flats in
which my family lived was hit and destroyed by a VI 'flying
bomb' in June 1944. It was rebuilt after the war and there I
was born and brought up. The war did not seem such a long
time ago and I read everything I could about it, starting with
battle action comic books and then graduating to more
serious stuff. One image that stuck with me – I think it was
from a school textbook – was a picture of Paulus surrendering at Stalingrad. It was juxtaposed with pictures of the
street-fighting in Stalingrad and of Red Army soldiers

advancing across the steppe. The caption read: Victory at Stalingrad.

The present book grew out of a suggestion by Heather McCallum, Humanities Editor in Chief at Pearson Education, that I should attempt to emulate Richard Overy's achievement in *The Battle* (2000) and write a succinct but authoritative and up-to-date 'story-book' about an important event of the Second World War. For me, no story of the Second World War was more important or fascinating than Stalingrad – a conviction that grew and matured as I researched and wrote the book.

I was greatly aided in my task by the comments and amendments of a number of people who read all or part of the draft manuscript: Edward Acton, Albert Axell, Michael Carley, Michael Cosgrave, Mark Harrison, Robert Service and Chris Ward. Dennis Ogden was, as always, encouraging and supportive and lent me some invaluable texts as well as commenting on the draft. David Glantz – to whose own work I owe a very great debt – was kind enough to supply me with some important Soviet documents. A special thanks, too, to Svetlana Frolova for checking and greatly improving my translation of the two Russian documents in the appendix to this text. Needless to say, any remaining errors in these texts, or in any other part of the book, are strictly my own responsibility. For stylistic reasons I have sometimes committed the deliberate error of writing about 'Russia' and the 'Russians', when strictly speaking I should have referred to the Soviet Union (or USSR) and to the Soviet people. The Russians – the majority population of the USSR – played by far the greatest role in the battle of Stalingrad and in winning the war on the Eastern Front. But indispensable to their victory were the Ukrainians, the Belorussians, the Armenians, the Azeris, the Balts, the Georgians and all the other groups of the multi-national, multi-ethnic Soviet Union that fought the Germans.

This is the sixth book on which I have collaborated with my partner, Celia Weston, and I am beginning to run out of superlatives to describe the value of her editorial and intellectual input. Let's just say that my demands on her were unusually intense this time and that her contribution was even more outstanding than is normally the case.

This book would not have been possible without the assistance of the inter-library loans section of University College Cork, who ordered scores of books for me from libraries in Britain, Ireland and the United States. Equally important was the privilege I had in trying out my ideas on Stalingrad in the UCC Department of History undergraduate seminar on the Second World War run by Michael Cosgrave and myself.

The book is dedicated to Geoff Weston, my late father-in-law. Geoff was a conscientious objector during World War II, and he served time in prison for his beliefs. He knew the meaning of commitment to a cause – the essential human ingredient of the struggle at Stalingrad. And, he would, I am sure, have been delighted with the irony of a 'war book' dedicated to his memory.

Finally, a word about the figures that liberally adorn the text. I have adopted a policy of rounding out the numbers. This makes the text easier to read and since really accurate statistics are hard to come by, and often contradictory, my most important task was to convey a sense of the scale of the fighting and of its costs and casualties.

ACKNOWLEDGEMENTS

We are grateful to the following for permission to reproduce copyright material:

Map 3 after map in *Stopped in Stalingrad*, University Press of Kansas (Hayward, J. S. A. 1998); Map 4 after map in *The Second World War* by John Keegan, published by Hutchinson. Used by permission of The Random House Group Ltd; Map 6 after map in *Zhukov's Greatest Defeat*, University Press of Kansas (Glantz, D. M. 1999); Map 11 after map in *The Battle of Kursk*, University Press of Kansas (Glantz, D. M. and House, J. M. 1999).

In some instances we have been unable to trace the owners of copyright material, and we would appreciate any information that would enable us to do so.

A CHRONOLOGY OF THE BATTLE OF STALINGRAD, 1942-3

5 April 1942:	Hitler Directive No.41 on the German offensive in Southern Russia
24 April 1942:	Alexander M. Vasilevskii takes over as Chief of the Soviet General Staff (formally appointed to the post 26 June 1942)
12 May 1942:	Beginning of the Soviet offensive at Kharkov
17 May 1942:	The Germans counter-attack at Kharkov
23–28 May 1942:	Encirclement and destruction of Soviet armies involved in the Kharkov battle
28 June 1942:	Beginning of the German offensive in Southern Russia
1–4 July 1942:	Fall of Sevastopol to Germans
6 July 1942:	Voronezh on the Don captured by the Germans
9 July 1942:	German Army Group South command split between Army Group A and Army Group B
12 July 1942:	Formation of 'Stalingrad Front' Soviet army group

23–24 July 1942:	German forces take Rostov-on-Don
23 July 1942:	Hitler Directive No.45 orders simultaneous main offensives on Stalingrad and towards the Caucasus
28 July 1942:	Stalin issues Order No.227 ('Not a step back')
9 August 1942:	Maikop oil field captured by the Germans
19 August 1942:	Paulus orders 6th Army to advance on Stalingrad
23–24 August 1942:	Mass German bombing of Stalingrad
25 August 1942:	Soviets declare Stalingrad to be in a state of siege
26 August 1942:	Zhukov appointed Deputy Supreme Commander of the Soviet Armed Forces
3 September 1942:	German troops attack outskirts of Stalingrad
10 September 1942:	Germans reach the Volga and split the 62nd and 64th Soviet Armies
12 September 1942:	Chuikov takes command of the 62nd Army
13 September 1942:	Beginning of the battle for Stalingrad city centre
13–14 September 1942:	Rodimtsev's 13th Guards Division

	begins crossing of Volga to Stalingrad
24 September 1942:	Halder replaced by Zeitzler as Chief of the Army General Staff
26 September 1942:	Most of central Stalingrad in German hands
9 October 1942:	System of dual political-military command in the Red Army (the Institution of Commissars) abolished
14 October 1942:	Climax of the German effort to take Stalingrad
8 November 1942:	Hitler announces in Munich that Stalingrad is in his hands
11 November 1942:	Last major German offensive in Stalingrad
19 November 1942:	Beginning of the Soviet counter-offensive ('Operation Uranus')
23 November 1942:	German 6th Army encircled in Stalingrad
24 November 1942:	Hitler orders the 6th Army to fight on in Stalingrad
25 November 1942:	Beginning of Soviet offensive against Army Group Centre ('Operation Mars')
25 November 1942:	Beginning of German airlift to Stalingrad

30 November 1942:	Paulus promoted to Colonel-General
12 December 1942:	Beginning of German 'Operation Wintergewitter' to rescue the 6th Army
16 December 1942:	Soviets launch 'Operation Little Saturn'
20 December 1942:	Operation Mars aborted
23 December 1942:	German relief operation to Stalingrad called off
28 December 1942:	German Army Group A ordered to retreat from Caucasus
8 January 1943:	Soviet ultimatum to 6th Army to surrender
10 January 1943:	Beginning of Soviet operations against the encircled 6th Army
17 January 1943:	Repeat of Soviet surrender ultimatum
25 January 1943:	Further Soviet offer of surrender terms
30 January 1943:	Paulus promoted to Field-Marshal
31 January 1943:	Surrender of Paulus and the 6th Army
2 February 1943:	Surrender of remaining German forces in Stalingrad

MAPS

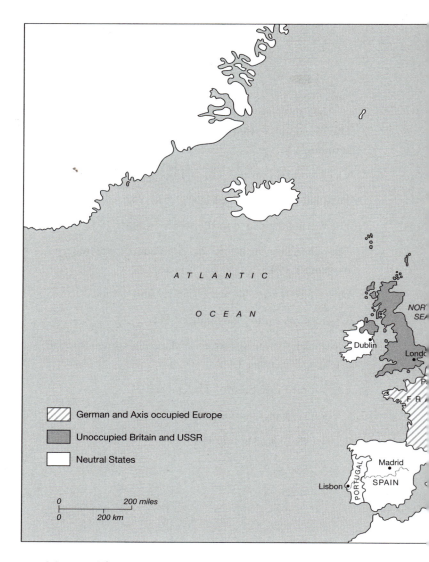

Map 1: The maximum extent of German expansion in Europe, autumn 1942

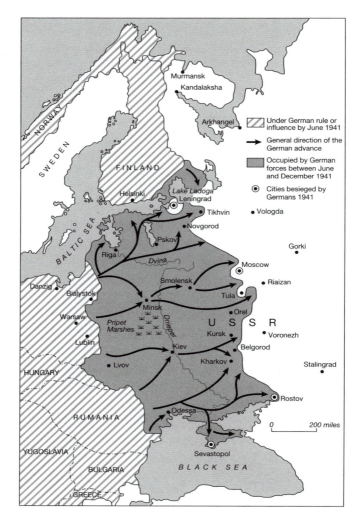

Map 2: 'Operation Barbarossa', June – December 1941

Source: after map in Arnold-Foster, M. (1973) *The World at War*, p. 128.

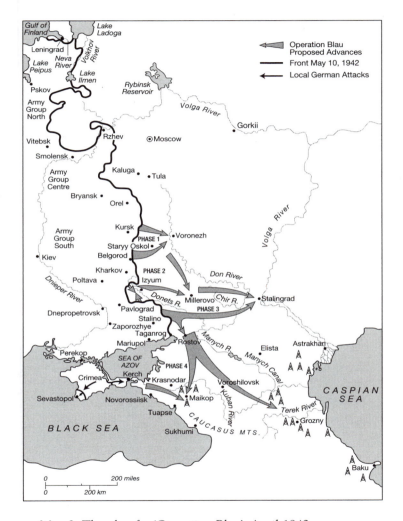

Map 3: The plan for 'Operation Blau', April 1942

Source: after map in *Stopped in Stalingrad*, University Press of Kansas (Hayward, J. S. A. 1998).

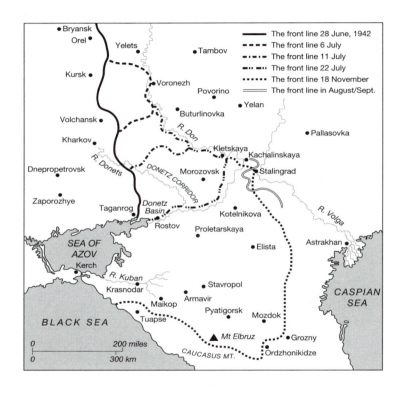

Map 4: The German advance in the south, summer 1942

Source: after map in *The Second World War* by John Keegan, published by Hutchinson. Used by permission of The Random House Group Ltd.

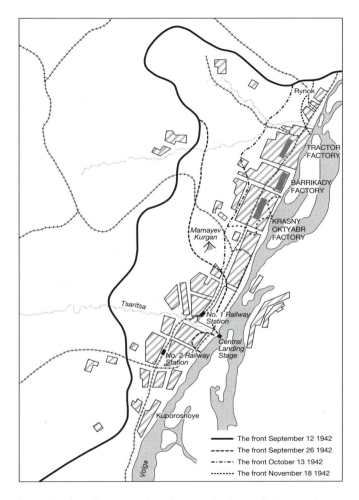

Map 5: The changing frontline at Stalingrad, September –
November 1942

Source: after map in Jukes, G. (1968) *Stalingrad*, p. 99.

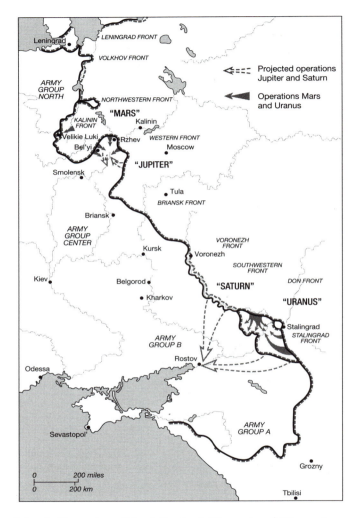

Map 6: Operations 'Mars', 'Jupiter', 'Saturn' and 'Uranus'

Source: after map in *Zhukov's Greatest Defeat*, University Press of Kansas (Glantz, D. M. 1999).

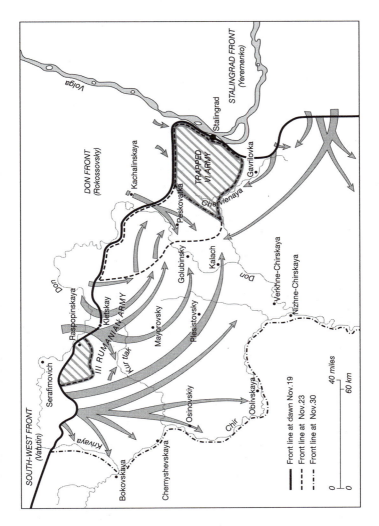

Map 7: 'Operation Uranus', November 1942

Source: after map in Jukes, G. (1968) *Stalingrad*, p. 123.

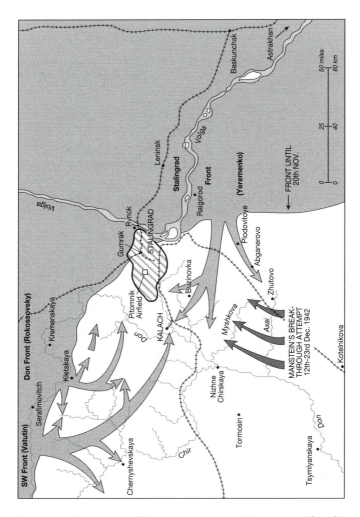

Map 8: 'Operation Wintergewitter' – Manstein's break-through attempt, December 1942

Source: after map in Werth, A. (1965) *Russia at War*, p. 452.

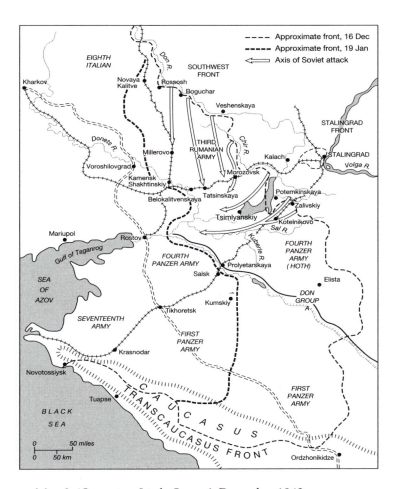

Map 9: 'Operation Little Saturn', December 1942

Source: after map in Bauer, M. E. and Ziemke, E. F. *Moscow to Stalingrad*, p. 486.

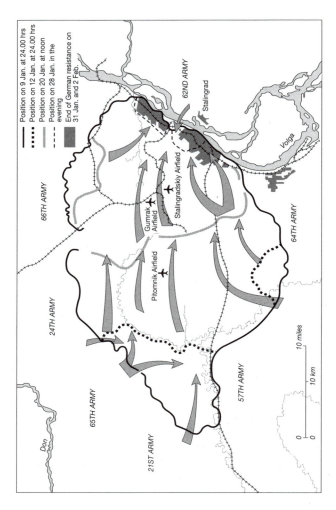

Map 10: 'Operation Ring', January 1943

Source: after map in Boog et al (2001) *Germany and the Second World War*, p. 1168.

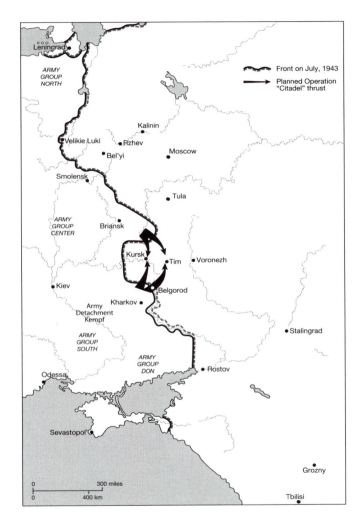

Map 11: The battle of Kursk, July 1943

Source: after map in *The Battle of Kursk*, University Press of Kansas (Glantz, D. M. and House, J. M. 1999).

chapter one

INTRODUCTION:

battle of the century

No battle of the Second World War has captured the public imagination as much as the clash between Soviet Russia and Nazi Germany at Stalingrad in 1942. For 60 years the story of this battle for the city on the Volga has been told and retold in countless histories, documentaries, novels and films. The source of this eternal fascination is not hard to discern. Stalingrad was an epic battle unmatched by any other in its dimensions, drama and decisiveness.

Contemporary observers of the battle – American and British, German and Russian – had no doubt that they were witnessing *the* crucial encounter of the Second World War. In August 1942 an editorial in *The Times* informed its readers that the Germans were making a supreme effort to reach Stalingrad and argued that 'the main theatre of the war is Russia . . . It is in Russia that events count most and will most deeply affect the future progress and even the final result of the war'. The front-page headlines of *The Times* that summer and autumn of 1942 reveal a dramatic story that gripped the world daily:

31 August: 'No quarter before Stalingrad'
4 September: 'Germans closing in on Stalingrad'
5 September: 'Ferocious battle outside Stalingrad'
7 September: 'Russians holding firm at Stalingrad
10 September: 'Costly German advance on Stalingrad'
12 September: 'Stalingrad to be held at all costs
14 September: 'Stalingrad fights back step by step'
16 September: 'Assault on Stalingrad intensified'
17 September: 'Stalingrad beats off many attacks'
18 September: 'Fighting in the streets of Stalingrad'
21 September: 'Street-by-street fight for Stalingrad'

28 September: 'Night and day battle at Stalingrad'

2 October: 'Attack after attack on Stalingrad'

3 October: 'Check to the Germans at Stalingrad'

9 October: 'Stalingrad defenders holding firm'

19 October: 'Critical battle for Stalingrad'.

When the battle was over Allied opinion was unanimous that the Soviets had not just won a great victory; they had turned back the Axis tide which had reached a high point of conquest and occupation in mid-1942 (see Map 1, p.xviii–xix). In Britain, the press lauded the Soviet victory at Stalingrad as nothing less than the salvation of European civilisation. In the United States a *New York Times* editorial of 4 February 1943 was grandiloquent but apt:

> 'Stalingrad is the scene of the costliest and most stubborn struggle in this war. The battle fought there to its desperate finish may turn out to be among the decisive battles in the long history of war … In the scale of its intensity, its destructiveness and its horror, Stalingrad has no parallel. It engaged the full strength of the two biggest armies in Europe and could fit into no lesser framework than that of a life-and-death conflict which encompasses the earth.'

Faced with many more hard battles to fight, the Soviet spin on Stalingrad was that the great victory had been won by the unbreakable unity and determination of the Russian peoples, their army and, of course, their leader – Joseph Stalin. In Germany, Nazi propagandists presented the lost battle as a heroic but necessary sacrifice, while at the same time doing all they could to cover up the scale of the defeat.

But there was no escaping the significance of the three days of national mourning that followed the German surrender at Stalingrad in February 1943.

The German summer campaign of 1942 was Hitler's last major strategic offensive, his last real chance of winning the Second World War. At Stalingrad the strategic initiative passed to the Soviets, and they never lost it. The road from Stalingrad did not lead directly to Berlin. There were many more battles and campaigns for the Soviets to fight and win (and sometimes lose). But after Stalingrad the question was when and how the war would be won, not whether it would be won.

Fifty years after its conclusion the great battle had lost none of its allure. In the late 1990s Antony Beevor's *Stalingrad* sold half a million copies worldwide, while the battle bestseller of an earlier generation, William Craig's *Enemy at the Gates*, inspired a major motion picture about the contest between German and Soviet snipers in the city.

Like many of the films and documentaries, much of the attention in the literature has focused on the desperate struggle for the city itself. But Stalingrad is a story of a campaign as well as a city battle. Having failed to conquer Soviet Russia in his *Blitzkrieg* campaign of 1941, Hitler set out to acquire the means to conduct a long war of attrition on the Eastern Front in summer 1942. Above all, that meant oil: the protection of existing German oil resources in Rumania, the capture of the oil fields of the Caucasus deep in the Soviet south, and the denial of oil supplies to Central and Northern Russia.

Ironically, Stalingrad was not really the main target of Operation Blau (Blue), the German campaign in Southern Russia that began in June 1942 (see Map 3, p.xxi). The Germans advanced on Stalingrad aiming not so much to take the city, as to destroy the Soviet armies in the territory between the great Don and Volga rivers. By August, however, capturing 'the city of Stalin' had become the pivot of the German campaign on the Eastern Front. The city's strategic location on the Volga meant that its capture by the Germans would cut Soviet supplies from the Baku oil fields – by far the most important source of fuel for Stalin's war machine. Having taken Stalingrad, the plan was to establish a defensive position that would enable the redeployment of German forces to an ongoing campaign in the Caucasus. And since Soviet forces defending the Caucasus would also have been isolated by the capture of Stalingrad, victory in the oil war – the main German goal of the southern campaign – would then be in sight.

In addition to strategy, psychology and symbolism played an important part in the battle and its outcome. Stalingrad's former name was Tsaritsyn. In 1918–19, during the Russian civil war, the future Soviet leader, Joseph Stalin, organised the defence of the city against counter-revolutionary armies seeking to overthrow the Bolshevik regime which had seized power in Russia in 1917. When Stalin succeeded Lenin as the leader of the Soviet Communist Party in the 1920s, the city was renamed in his honour. The capture of Stalingrad by the Germans would have been a severe blow to the Soviet leader's prestige, as well as denying him access to his oil.

The problem was that Stalingrad did not fall to the Germans. By October 1942 most of the city was in German hands, but a heroic Soviet defence saved the city from complete enemy occupation. Crucially, control of the Volga remained in Soviet hands and Soviet supplies continued to flow across the river to the embattled Red Army defenders of Stalingrad holding out in a few square miles of rubble in what had once had been a city. The aim of Operation Blau had been to draw the Soviet forces into open battle and to destroy them. Instead, the Germans found themselves drawn into a costly, exhausting and ultimately disastrous war of attrition in the ruins of Stalingrad.

Meanwhile, the Soviets had been preparing their counter-stroke. In November 1942 the Red Army launched a massive counter-offensive which broke through the German flanks north and south of the city and encircled the German 6th Army in Stalingrad. In December the Germans attempted to rescue the 6th Army by a breakthrough operation from outwith the Soviet encirclement. When this failed, Hitler fell back on air supply for delivery of essential support and provisions to the trapped 6th Army. The *Luftwaffe* flew many thousands of missions but supplies ran far short of the hundreds of tons of food, ammunition and medical supplies required daily by the quarter of a million troops inside the *Kessel* (or cauldron, as the Germans called the encircled area of their forces in Stalingrad). In January 1943 the Soviets renewed their offensive, this time aiming to liquidate the *Kessel*. The emaciated, demoralised and disease-ridden defenders of the *Kessel* were no match for the seven Soviet armies which rapidly reduced the *Kol'tso* (the ring) as the Soviets called it.

On 31 January the Soviets captured the commander of the 6th Army, Field Marshal Fredrich Paulus – the highest ranking of the 24 German generals who surrendered at Stalingrad. Two days later the remaining German forces in Stalingrad capitulated.

The loss of the 6th Army – an elite fighting force of the German army – was catastrophic enough. It was the biggest and most traumatic defeat in German military history and the myth of the invincible *Wehrmacht* was gone forever. But the overall strategic picture was even worse. By the end of the Stalingrad campaign Germany and its Axis allies on the Eastern Front had suffered casualties of a million and a half dead, wounded and captured. Nearly 50 divisions – almost the whole of five armies – had been lost. In the Caucasus, the German armies beat a rapid retreat north and barely escaped entrapment themselves. In the central sector, in front of Moscow, German Army Group Centre survived a major Soviet offensive launched simultaneously with the one at Stalingrad, but took heavy casualties and the threat of renewed Russian attack remained. In the north the Germans still surrounded Leningrad, as they had done since 1941, but in January 1943 the land blockade was breached and it was only a matter of time before the siege of the Soviet Union's second city would be completely lifted. By spring 1943 the Germans were outnumbered two to one on the Eastern Front and outgunned many more times over. In the summer the Germans attempted to stabilise their defensive position by launching a great tank offensive at Kursk in the central sector, but this was another battle they lost, and it was one from which their famed Panzer forces never recovered.

The Soviets paid a high price for their victories. The Stalingrad campaign alone cost an estimated 2.5 million casualties. But no-one, either at the time or subsequently, seriously doubted that it was worth it. The Soviet victory at Stalingrad was *the* turning point in the war on the Eastern Front and the Eastern Front was the main front of the Second World War. More than 80 per cent of all combat during the Second World War took place on the Eastern Front. The Germans suffered in excess of 90 per cent of their total war losses on the Eastern Front: 600 divisions destroyed by the Soviets; ten million dead, wounded, missing or captured. As the war progressed the western Allied contribution to the land war in Europe grew proportionately. Following the D-Day landings of June 1944, the American, British, Canadian and other allies deployed a two million strong force in France against about a million German defenders. However, even in summer 1944 there were still twice as many Germans serving on the Eastern Front, as in western theatres.

The Germans blamed their defeat at Stalingrad on the vagaries of the weather, on the logistical difficulties of operating in the vast expanses of Russia, and, above all, on the seemingly inexhaustible Soviet manpower reserves. After the war, but not at the time, the favourite sport of retired German generals was attacking Hitler for his meddling in military affairs and his tactical and strategic errors in relation to Stalingrad and other campaigns.

Soviet propagandists, on the other hand, depicted Stalingrad as a triumph for the Soviet socialist system. The Soviet Union, they argued, had out-produced, out-fought and out-lasted Nazi Germany. Underlying that victory, they argued, was a superior socialist economic system, a dynamic political and military leadership and, above all, a people united in their determination to resist Nazi invasion, conquest and occupation.

Curiously, an inverse theme may be found in the writings of many anti-communist critics of the Soviet system. Their argument is that the Soviet system did indeed triumph at Stalingrad but only because it was authoritarian, brutal and ruthless, more so even than the Nazi regime. There is some truth in this, but it stretches credibility to believe that such a victory could have been achieved solely on the back of fear, discipline and regimentation. The Soviet regime dispensed plenty of that during the battle of Stalingrad, but it also inspired and organised an unparalleled heroic defence. Similarly, while Hitler and his generals made many critical mistakes, so did Stalin and the Soviets. Overall Soviet resources and reserves were superior to those of the Germans, but at many critical moments in the battle for Stalingrad the *Wehrmacht's* front-line forces and firepower were far greater than the Red Army's. German under-estimation of Soviet strength was a major factor in their defeat at Stalingrad, but there was nothing pre-ordained about the successful mobilisation and deployment of Soviet material superiority – that was a matter of effective politics and economics. The Soviets were able to maintain the morale of their armed forces in the most calamitous circumstances and to sustain a war mobilisation that produced the resources necessary to win the battle and, ultimately, the war. And, for all its ideological and political rigidities, the Soviet system was also able to foster a professional military leadership and officer corps that matched and then surpassed that of the *Wehrmacht*, the conqueror of continental Europe, most of North Africa and, in 1941–2, a good deal of Russia.

At the pinnacle of the Soviet system stood Stalin. During the war Stalin was Supreme Commander of the Armed Forces, Commissar for Defence and Chairman of the GKO (*Gosudarstvennyi Komitet Oborony* or State Defence Committee), whilst at the same time remaining head of the Communist Party and the government. No other war leader exercised as close and detailed control over all aspects of the war effort as did Stalin.

Unlike Hitler, Stalin has generally had a good press from his military commanders – at least from those who survived his dictatorship. In Soviet military memoirs there is much criticism of Stalin's failure to anticipate the German invasion in June 1941, a failure that was very costly in the early days of the war, and some complaint about his predilection for offensive rather than defensive action. More common, however, is testimony to his grasp of military strategy and doctrine, his command of the details of operations, the decisiveness and clarity of his decision making, and his willingness to accept professional advice. During the war Stalin was a team player, a leader with unchallengeable power, but one whose leadership fell far short of the over-powering domination and idiosyncrasy of Hitler.

Of course, Stalin was as brutal, ruthless and authoritarian as the system he presided over. He had no compunction about sacrificing huge numbers of lives in order to achieve his goals. His was the authority under which Soviet soldiers were executed for cowardice and desertion during the war, some 13,500 during the battle of Stalingrad alone. As the Germans advanced across Russia, Stalin ordered the execution of tens of thousands of political prisoners, lest they fall into the hands of the enemy. He was ruthless in the application of a 'scorched earth' policy as the Red Army retreated across Russia. He showed no hesitation in purging and punishing commanders who failed him. In July 1941 he ordered the execution of the commander of the Soviet Western Front, General Dmitrii Pavlov, blaming him for the initial success of the German invasion of Russia. Several members of Pavlov's staff perished with him. All of these officers were 'rehabilitated' after Stalin's death in 1953. On the other hand, Stalin was pragmatic enough to release from prison a number of disgraced and purged Red Army commanders, including General Konstantin K. Rokossovsky, who led the final Soviet assault on the Germans at Stalingrad.

As Richard Overy has said (1997, p.xvi), Stalin is easy to hate but difficult to understand and come to terms with. Whatever his crimes there is no gainsaying his role in the defeat of Hitler and the Nazis. At the time no one had any doubt about that. Indeed, during the war a cult of Stalin's leadership reigned not only in the Soviet Union but throughout the Allied world. In this respect Stalingrad was a turning point for Stalin too. In January 1943 Stalin was acclaimed Man of the Year 1942 by *Time* magazine (an honour bestowed on Hitler in 1938), while at home the legend of Stalin's military prowess and genius began to take root and grow. Before the war the cult of Stalin's personality had been extreme enough, but it was nothing compared with the heights it reached on the back of victories such as Stalingrad. Stalin emerged from the war in a virtually unassailable political position and as a figure of adulation at home and abroad. He used this power to reassert his dictatorial position, to re-subordinate the military to Communist Party control, and to marginalise many of the commanders who had won him such great victories. Not that such ingratitude seemed to impact much on their positive assessment of him as war leader, not even after he was long dead, buried and denounced by his erstwhile comrades in the Communist Party.

Hitler's historical fate was somewhat different. Stalingrad marked the beginning of the end of the invincible Hitler myth in Germany. After the war he was almost universally blamed for the defeat, despite the valiant efforts of some historians to arrive at a more balanced judgement. As we shall see, Hitler made many mistakes in the Stalingrad campaign, but they were not his alone. On many issues of grand strategy, particularly the economics, politics and psychology of the war, he had a firmer grasp of the issues than did his generals. As Bernd Wegner has pointed out, there is much more to the story of the Nazi dictator's role in the war than 'the cliché of Hitler's military dilettantism' (Boog et al, 2001, p.1117).

Stalingrad marked the climax of Hitler and Stalin's personal duel. But more important was the clash of the conflicting ideologies, polities and economies over which they presided. While Stalingrad was a battle – a contest of military forces, resources, strategies and tactics – it was also a political, economic, psychological and moral struggle. The result of that multi-dimensional struggle changed the course and outcome of the Second World War and shaped much of the peace that followed. According to John Erickson: 'if the battle of Poltava in 1709 turned Russia into a European power, then Stalingrad set the Soviet Union on the road to being a world power' (1983, p.43).

Stalin won and Hitler lost. But it was a close call. There were many times during the campaign and the battle for the city when decisions and actions by both sides could have changed fundamentally the course of events. Stalingrad is a classic case-study of the role of chance, circumstances and, above all, personality in the making of history. We know what happened eventually, but we also know that things could have turned out very differently. Even in retrospect the battle retains its indeterminate character. Stalingrad is one of those epic stories that sustains its tension and drama through to the very end.

chapter two

WAR OF ANNIHILATION:

the German campaign in Russia, 1941–2

The German invasion of Soviet Russia in June 1941 was the greatest military operation the world had ever seen. Just before dawn on Sunday 22 June, 170 German and Axis divisions attacked across a 1000-mile front. The 3.5 million strong invasion force was organised in three massed army groups: Army Group North attacked from East Prussia and fought its way along the Baltic coastal lands towards Leningrad; Army Group Centre advanced towards Minsk, Smolensk and Moscow; while Army Group South headed for the Ukraine and its capital, Kiev (see Map 2, p.xx).

The Germans employed much the same *Blitzkrieg* tactics as they had in 1939–40 when invading Poland, France and the Low Countries. Concentrated columns of powerful armoured divisions punched their way through enemy defences and encircled Soviet forces from the rear. Infantry divisions, whose task it was to destroy the encircled enemy forces and hold captured territory, followed the German Panzers.

The German plan of campaign was rapid conquest of European Russia and the establishment of a defensive line running from Arkhangel in the north towards Astrakhan in the south. That meant achieving an advance into the Soviet Union to a depth of more than 1000 miles. It was an ambitious plan, but the Germans expected to win the war in the USSR in a matter of weeks, and certainly before the onset of winter brought an end to large-scale operations. German optimism that a rapid victory could be won in Russia was, in part, a political calculation about the internal weakness of the communist regime. As Hitler said: 'you only have to kick in the door and the whole rotten structure will come crashing down'.

Certainly, the initial German attack was spectacularly successful. Defending the USSR's frontier was an equally strong Soviet force. But the Red Army, caught by surprise, was unprepared and unable to absorb the weight of the massive German attack. On the first day the Germans wiped out most of the Soviet airforce. By 3 July the Chief of the German Army General Staff, General Franz Halder, was claiming in his diary that it was 'probably no overstatement to say that the Russian campaign has been won in the space of two weeks'. Within three weeks the Soviets had suffered three-quarters of a million casualties and lost 10,000 tanks and 4000 aircraft. Within three months the Germans had captured Kiev, virtually encircled Leningrad and were poised to attack Moscow. By the end of 1941 the Soviets had lost 200 divisions in battle and suffered a stunning 4.3 million casualties, dead, wounded, missing or captured.

By autumn 1941 the Soviet state stood on the very brink of collapse and defeat. In October 1941, Army Group Centre launched Operation Typhoon, an attack on Moscow by more than 70 divisions – a million men, with 1700 tanks, 14,000 artillery pieces and almost 1000 planes. The attack brought the Germans to within 20 miles of the Soviet capital, but then came one of the great turning points of the Second World War. The *Wehrmacht* failed to take Moscow and its invasion ground to a halt along the whole of the Eastern Front. On 5 December the Soviets launched a major counter-attack in front of Moscow. Now it was Army Group Centre's turn to retreat, although Hitler quickly ordered a policy of no withdrawal and this steadied the German line. In January 1942 Stalin ordered an ambitious general counter-offensive along the whole of the Eastern Front. The aim was to destroy Army Group Centre and to roll back the German invasion force along a broad front. In February Stalin called upon the Red Army 'to make 1942 the year of the final rout of the German-fascist troops and the liberation of the Soviet land from the Hitlerite blackguards!'. But by this time the Soviet counter-offensive had ground to a halt. The Germans had been pushed 40–50 miles back from the positions they had held on the outskirts of Moscow but here, as elsewhere on the Eastern Front, they retained control of almost all the territory they had conquered in 1941. The Soviets had won a crucial tactical battle in front of Moscow but their dreams of a successful strategic counter-offensive did not materialise at this time. Still, the immediate threat to Moscow had been lifted and that fact alone signalled the end of the German ambition to conquer Russia in the course of a single, lightning campaign.

The codename for the German invasion of the Soviet Union was Operation Barbarossa in honour of Frederick I ('Red Beard'), the Holy Roman Emperor who led a 12th century crusade to liberate Christianity's holy places from Muslim control. According to Nazi propaganda the German campaign in Russia was of a similar character. Germany, it was claimed, had attacked the USSR to pre-empt a Soviet strike against the Reich, and was now leading a crusade against the unholy Bolshevik empire that threatened European civilisation.

In terms of self-image and self-belief there was an important element of authenticity in this propaganda legend. The Nazi regime was genuinely and fundamentally anti-communist and really did perceive the Soviet regime as the embodiment of a Bolshevik, revolutionary threat to European culture. It is also true that the Soviet Union, which had the largest armed forces in the world, was viewed as a strategic threat to German domination of continental Europe. But, contrary to the claims of some authors, Stalin had no plan or intention to attack Germany. Indeed, until the very day of the invasion the Soviets were striving to maintain the non-aggression treaty that had been signed with the Germans in August 1939. The initiative and decision for war was indubitably Hitler's alone.

The German dictator's decision to invade Russia was the biggest of his life and the one that led ultimately to the downfall of the Nazi regime. Historians have long discussed Hitler's motives for this action and the complex decision-making process which lead to Barbarossa. But the outline of what happened was pretty simple and straightforward.

In August 1939 Hitler had signed a non-aggression treaty with Stalin to secure his eastern flank from attack before Germany became involved in a war with Britain and France over Poland. Poland was under threat from Germany because of a dispute about the so-called 'Polish Corridor'. This was a strip of territory which gave the Poles access to the Baltic, but which cut off East Prussia from the main part of Germany and gave the Polish authorities customs control of the German city-port of Danzig. As early as April 1939, Hitler had decided to resolve this dispute by invading and occupying Poland. Britain and France, however, were pledged by treaty to defend Poland from German attack. In those circumstances Hitler put aside his ideological hostility to Bolshevik Russia and instead sought a protective deal with Stalin.

The Soviets, too, put aside their hostility to Nazi Germany. A deal with Hitler suited Stalin, who feared that the USSR would be dragged into a war in defence of Poland while the British and French stood on the sidelines and reaped the benefits of a destructive Soviet-German war. Hitler, on the other hand, offered the Soviets a share in the spoils of war, including the right to occupy Eastern Poland and to control the Baltic States. The deal was encapsulated in a secret protocol to the non-aggression pact signed between the two countries on 23 August 1939: Russian neutrality towards Germany in return for Soviet political and territorial gains in Eastern Europe.

On 1 September 1939 Germany invaded Poland. This was the trigger for a war that was eventually to embroil most of the world. As promised, the Soviet Union remained neutral. Then, on 17 September the USSR joined in the attack on Poland and occupied Western Belorussia and Western Ukraine – lands of the former Russian Tsarist empire which Moscow had claimed as its own since the 1920s. This move was followed by the incorporation of Estonia, Latvia and Lithuania into a Soviet sphere of influence in the Baltic. The only hiccup in the Soviet expansionary programme was Finnish resistance to incorporation into Moscow's sphere. This resulted in a Soviet attack on Finland in December 1939 and the beginning of the so-called 'Winter War'. By March 1940 the Soviets had forced the Finns to accept terms for peace, but the Red Army suffered substantial casualties during the war, including 40,000 dead, and its reputation as a fighting force took a severe battering in the face of heroic Finnish resistance. Throughout the Soviet-Finnish conflict the Germans maintained a strict neutrality, despite pleas for their intercession made by Finland and other states.

In 1939–40 the Soviet-German compact suited Hitler very well. The conquest of Poland in September 1939 was followed in spring 1940 by the invasion of Norway, Denmark, Belgium, Holland, Luxembourg and France. The fall of France in June 1940 established German predominance on the European continent and presaged a further bout of expansion in 1940–1, this time in Eastern Europe and the Balkans. It was during this period that the 'Axis' alliance between Germany and Italy was extended to Hungary, Rumania, and Bulgaria. It was this development that brought Germany into conflict with the Soviet Union. Politically and diplomatically, Moscow resisted German encroachments in the Balkans, particularly in Bulgaria, and in Yugoslavia, which the Germans invaded in April 1941.

By the end of 1940 Hitler had become disillusioned about the deal with Stalin and saw the USSR no longer as an ally but as a challenger. It was against this background that Hitler authorised Führer Directive No.21 of 18 December 1940 – the order to make preparations for Operation Barbarossa. One of the staff officers involved in implementing this directive was General Fredrich Paulus, later to command the 6th Army at Stalingrad.

The planned invasion was to some extent a straightforward military operation. Enemy forces would be attacked and destroyed and enemy territory conquered and occupied. But the German invasion of Russia turned out to be a far from normal military operation. It was, as Ernst Nolte put it, 'the most horrendous war of conquest, enslavement and annihilation that the modern world has ever seen.' (Müller and Ueberschär, 1997, p.76.)

What emerged during the preparation of Operation Barbarossa was a plan for *Vernichtungskrieg* – a war of destruction, of extermination. Not only the Red Army, but also the entire Soviet communist regime was to be destroyed. And the anti-communism of the Nazis was of a very specific bent: it was racist. According to the Nazis' anti-Semitic ideology the Soviet Union was a *judeobolshevik* state – a communist regime under Jewish control and influence. Its destruction required the extermination of the Jewish cadres and Jewish influence that defined the essence of the Soviet state and the threat it posed to the Aryan culture of Germany.

Nazi racist ideology also defined the Slavic peoples of Russia and Eastern Europe as an inferior race of *Untermenschen* or sub-humans. The Slavs were not initially slated for extermination or expulsion (at least not all of them) but they were destined for servitude and slavery. As Hitler said later: 'our guiding principle is that the existence of these people is justified only by their economic exploitation for our benefit.'

The Nazi attitude towards the Slavs was reflected in economic planning for Barbarossa. German armies invading Russia would live off the land and off local produce and labour. Soviet territories were to be plundered for food, raw materials and industrial products for shipment back to Germany. In the longer term there would be large-scale colonisation of Russia by German settlers in search of *Lebensraum* ('living space'), which would necessitate the expulsion of millions of native peoples to Siberia or elsewhere. Conquered Russia would also be used as a dumping ground for Jews and other 'inferior races' of which the Germans wanted to rid Europe. At this time the Nazis' 'final solution' of the Jewish question in Europe was seen by them in terms of the mass expulsion of the Jews to the east, not their mass murder – not yet anyway.

The war that Hitler planned to launch against Russia was an ideological war against communism and a race war against the Jews and the Slavs. What that would mean in practice was made quite clear by Hitler in a speech to his generals on 30 March 1941: 'The war against Russia will be such that it cannot be conducted in a knightly fashion; the struggle is one of ideologies and racial differences and will have to be conducted with unprecedented, unmerciful and unrelenting harshness.' This was much more than mere rhetoric, as various practical preparations for a war of annihilation show.

In March 1941 agreement was reached between the *Wehrmacht* and the SS on the role of the *Einsatzgruppen*. These were special 'action teams' of the SS that were to follow the German armies into Russia and eliminate judeobolshevik officials, activists and intellectuals. This was a momentous decision. It is unlikely that the *Einsatzgruppen* were from the very beginning intended to be the instrument of an indiscriminate Holocaust of Jews in Russia, but this is certainly what they shortly became.

On 13 May Hitler issued a decree which effectively exempted German soldiers from punishment for any atrocities they might commit in Russia, except where issues of Army discipline were at stake. A few days later the *Wehrmacht* issued some 'Guidelines for the behaviour of the fighting forces in Russia':

'1. Bolshevism is the mortal enemy of the National Socialist German people. Germany's struggle is aimed against that disruptive ideology and its exponents.
2. That struggle demands ruthless and energetic action against Bolshevik agitators, guerrillas, saboteurs, Jews and the complete liquidation of any active or passive resistance.
3. Extreme reserve and most alert vigilance are called for towards all members of the Red Army – even prisoners – as treacherous methods of fighting are to be expected. The Asiatic soldiers of the Red Army in particular are inscrutable, unpredictable, insidious and unfeeling.' (Boog et al, 1998, pp.514–15)

On 6 June the Wehrmacht issued 'Guidelines on the treatment of commissars'. This was the infamous 'Commissar Order', which dealt with the fate of commissars – the political officers of the Red Army – who 'if captured in battle, or while resisting, are as a matter of principle to be finished off with the weapons at once' (*ibid.*, p.510).

What these completely illegal and criminal orders envisaged

was a savage but still limited and controlled campaign to eliminate the key personnel of the Soviet state. As Jürgen Förster points out, the campaign was a partnership in which 'there was to be a division of responsibility between the army and the SS ... While the SS was charged with elimination of the civilian cadres of the inimical *Weltanschauung*, the army was to eliminate the "Jewish-Bolshevik intelligentsia" within the Red Army, the commissars, and the real or potential carriers of resistance.' (Cesarani, 1994, p.89)

The projected scenario was nightmarish enough. What actually happened was infinitely worse. The implementation of the planned war of destruction soon escalated into the mass murder of Soviet soldiers and citizens by the SS and the *Wehrmacht*. It was this escalation of the war that made the struggle on the Eastern Front so barbarous, not the extent or brutality of the combat, or even the abnormal level of the 'normal' atrocities committed by the troops of both sides to the conflict.

During the course of Operation Barbarossa in 1941, the Germans killed hundreds of thousands of Soviet soldiers in combat. However, most Soviet losses consisted of prisoners captured as a result of the successful encirclement operations conducted by the German panzer divisions. In the encirclement of Minsk, the Germans bagged 400,000 Soviet prisoners and at Smolensk another 300,000. In the Kiev encirclement, a half million Soviet soldiers were caught and another half million fell into German hands at Briansk and Viazma. By the end of 1941 the Germans had taken literally millions of Soviet POWs. By February 1942, however, two million out of the three million Soviets taken prisoner in

1941 were dead from starvation, disease and maltreatment. After this time the death rates in the camps began to decrease, as the Germans put the prisoners to work rather than let them die of neglect. Nevertheless, during the course of the whole war the Germans captured nearly six million Soviet POWs, of whom more than half died in captivity. (The issue of Soviet treatment of German POWs is dealt with in Chapter 5.)

The attrition of the Soviet POWs is mainly a story of brutal carelessness and callous treatment underwritten by a racist ideology which designated them as less than human. But the Germans also systematically murdered certain categories of Soviet prisoner. Not long after the outbreak of the war the SS negotiated an agreement with the German army to enable the *Einsatzgruppen* to weed out so-called 'intolerable elements' among Soviet POWs. This meant killing all captured Jews, party and state functionaries, and intellectuals – an estimated 140,000 in all between 1941 and 1945. Perhaps the most infamous instance of this mass murder was the 'test' gassing of 600 Soviet POWs at Auschwitz in September 1941 – the prototype of the killing method later adopted to exterminate millions of Jews in German concentration camps throughout occupied Poland and Russia. In fact, Auschwitz, like many of the other camps, was originally built by, and for, Soviet POWs, not the Jews who arrived later.

But the connection between Operation Barbarossa and the Holocaust – the mass murder of European Jewry – was more than merely technical and contingent. The Holocaust began on the Eastern Front and grew out of the German

Vernichtungskrieg – the war of destruction. In the Soviet territories invaded and occupied by the Germans, there were three million Jews. About two million of them were massacred by the Germans during the course of the war, most of them in 1941–2. The main instruments of this campaign of extermination were the *Einsatzgruppen*, which accompanied each of the three German Army groups into action. At first, the kill-rate of the SS action teams numbered hundreds and, at most, thousands, which reflected a relatively selective policy aimed mainly at able-bodied Jewish men, all of whom were deemed actual or potential threats to Nazi rule. By autumn 1941, however, the policy had changed to the wholesale slaughter of Jewish communities and the body count rose to the hundreds of thousands. Symbolising the moment of transition was the Babi Yar massacre at the end of September 1941.

Babi Yar, a ravine outside Kiev, was where the SS shot dead more than 30,000 Jews over the course of two days, ostensibly in retaliation for delayed action time-bombs exploded by the Soviets in the city centre. Babi Yar was later made famous by the Soviet poet Yevgeny Yevtushenko who, in the 1960s, criticised the absence of a Soviet war memorial at the site of the massacre. 'Over Babi Yar', he wrote, 'there are no memorials . . .

> The trees are threatening, look like judges.
> And everything is one silent cry.
> Taking my hat off
> I feel myself slowly going grey.
> And I am one silent cry

Over the many thousands of the buried;
Am every old man killed here,
Every child killed here . . .
No Jewish blood runs among my blood,
But I am as bitterly and hardly hated
By every anti-semite
As if I were a Jew. By this
I am a Russian.'
(1962, p.83–84)

Similar massacres of Jews were repeated by the *Einsatzgruppen* in villages, towns and cities all over the occupied Soviet territories. By December 1941 the number of SS victims was approaching half a million.

Indispensable to the successful functioning of the SS units as mass murder machines was the co-operation of the German armed forces. In the case of Babi Yar, for example, the massacre took place in an area occupied by the German 6th Army, which provided essential logistical support to the SS in the carrying out of the killings. A similar pattern of support was also evident shortly afterwards in the city of Kharkov, also controlled by the 6th Army, when 20,000 Jewish civilians perished at the hands of the SS.

The 6th Army's main claim to fame, however, is its later role in the struggle for Stalingrad. At this time it was commanded not by Paulus but by Field Marshal Walter von Reichenau, the author in October 1941 of one of the most notorious German army orders of the Eastern Front campaign. He informed the 6th Army that:

'The soldier in the east is not just a fighter according to the rules of the art of war, but also the bearer of an implacable national idea, and the avenger of all the bestialities inflicted on the German and related peoples. For that reason, the soldier must have full understanding of the need for a harsh but just punishment of Jewish subhumanity ... Irrespective of any political considerations of the future, the German soldier must achieve two things:

(1) the complete annihilation of the Bolshevik heresy, the Soviet state, and its armed forces;

(2) the merciless elimination of alien perfidy and atrocity, thereby securing the life of the German Wehrmacht in Russia. Only in this way can we fulfil our historic task of liberating the German people from the Asiatic-Jewish danger once and for all.' (Boog et al. 1998, p.1212)

Reichenau also stated: 'to supply local inhabitants and prisoners of war with food is an act of unnecessary humanity.' His attitudes were not unique among the German generals. In November 1941 General Hermann Hoth, commander of the 17th Army, issued his order on the 'conduct of the German soldiers in the east'. He informed his army:

'More strongly than ever, we carry in us the belief that this is the turning-point of an era in which the leadership of Europe is transferred to the German people by virtue of the superiority of its race and its achievements. We clearly recognise our mission to save European culture from the advance of Asiatic barbarism. We now know that we have to fight against an embittered and tenacious opponent. The struggle can only end with the annihilation of one or another; there can be no settlement

> ... Russia is not a European state, but an Asiatic state. Every step further into this bleak, enslaved land teaches us the difference. Europe, and especially Germany must be freed from this pressure, and from the destructive forces of Bolshevism, for all time'. (*ibid.*, pp.1214–15)

The 17th Army later took part in the campaign in the Caucasus, while Hoth himself was transferred to the command of the 4th Panzer Army, part of which fought in the battle for Stalingrad.

Another future hero of the Stalingrad campaign was General Erich von Manstein, commander of the 11th Army. He urged his men to understand 'the need for the harsh punishment of Jewry, the intellectual carrier of Bolshevik terror' and proclaimed that 'the Jewish-Bolshevik system must be wiped out once and for all. Never again must it interfere in our European living-space' (*ibid.*, pp.1215–16).

What these quotations show is the extent to which the German generals shared Nazi ideas, goals and, above all, the programme of Eastern expansion. By no means all of them were Nazis, but most embraced with enthusiasm Hitler's anti-communism, anti-Semitism and anti-Slavism.

After the war von Manstein and others attempted to justify their orders and their rhetoric by citing the need for harsh measures to counter the irregular warfare of Soviet partisans in the rear of the German armies. A large-scale Soviet partisan movement did develop as the war progressed and it did engage in a murderous struggle with the Germans and their collaborators. However, the Germans' repressive measures *predated* the mass development of the partisan movement and, indeed, largely inspired it. As Christian Streit notes the burning of villages and the execution of inhabitants became commonplace during the summer of 1941. In September 1941 the *Wehrmacht* issued orders that between 50 and 100 'communists' should be killed for every German who fell victim to partisan attack. During the period of Operation Barbarossa alone, the German army executed tens of thousands of Soviet civilians as partisans or suspected partisans.

There was close connection, a symbiosis even, between the anti-Jewish campaign of the SS and the supposed anti-partisan actions of the *Wehrmacht*. In the German mind all Jews were stigmatised as partisans and all partisans branded as Jews. 'The Jew is a partisan. The partisan is a Jew', was the German slogan on the Eastern Front in 1941. Such a mentality rationalised the mass murder of Soviet Jews, while at the same time legitimising harsh and indiscriminate anti-partisan measures.

In 1941 the Soviet authorities were not unaware of the scope of the tragedy unfolding in the occupied territories. Various reports of German atrocities were coming in from agents, partisans and escaped civilians and soldiers. In November 1941 Stalin stated publicly that 'the German-fascist invaders are plundering our country, destroying [our] towns and villages ... The Hitlerite hordes are murdering and outraging the peaceful inhabitants of our country, having no mercy on women, children or old people.' His rallying cry was that 'if the Germans want a war of extermination, they will get one.'

But it was only when the Soviets began to recapture territory in December 1941 that a clearer picture began to emerge of the extent of German pillage, destruction and atrocities. In January 1942 the Soviet government issued the first of many statements detailing 'the monstrous crimes, atrocities and acts of violence of the German-Fascist invaders'. These were propaganda statements, of course, but ones that actually underestimated the extent of the annihilatory war being waged by the Germans. In part, this underestimate was deliberate. There was a fine line between, on the one hand, arousing the population's anger and thirst for revenge and, on the other, encouraging horror and fear of the Germans. Nevertheless, by 1942 the Soviet people, particularly the soldiers at the front, could have no doubts about the character of the life and death struggle in which they were involved. Such knowledge and people's perceptions were a vital factor in the popular mobilisation to defeat the enemy when the Germans resumed their invasion campaign in summer 1942. Its importance is underlined by Robert Service, who argues:

> 'If it had not been for Hitler's fanatical racism, the USSR would not have won the struggle on the Eastern Front. Stalin's repressiveness towards his own citizens would have cost him the war against Nazi Germany, and the post-war history of the Soviet Union and the world would have been fundamentally different.' (1997, p.290)

During 1941, however, Soviet survival was a function not so much of utter desperation as of other military, political and economic factors. Among them was patriotic mobilisation – albeit by a repressive, authoritarian regime. From the very first days of the June invasion, the struggle against Germany was declared to be a patriotic war in defence of the motherland. Communist political ideology was downplayed and there was a revival of traditional, Russian nationalism. Proletarian international solidarity was overshadowed by calls for pan-Slavic unity in the face of a racist invader. There was a major religious revival as the Russian Orthodox Church was officially rehabilitated and enlisted in the war effort. In foreign policy terms, the war was defined as a war for freedom and liberation that would be fought in alliance with the western capitalist democracies of Britain and the United States.

Themes such as these were the basis of a successful political mobilisation by a regime that had never enjoyed more than minority support among the Soviet population. At the centre of this rallying of the people stood Stalin, a dictator, but *their* dictator.

Stalin's role in the early months of the war is controversial, like every other aspect of his life and career. For many years he was blamed for the initial success of the 'surprise' German attack on 22 June 1941. For months before the launch of Operation Barbarossa reports had been flooding into Moscow warning of a coming German attack, but Stalin chose to ignore the warnings and concentrated on maintaining peace with the Nazi regime rather than on mobilising for war against it.

Recent research, however, has revealed a complex political and diplomatic picture on the eve of Barbarossa. Stalin refused to believe that the Germans were going to attack imminently for a number of reasons. First, the Germans waged a highly successful deception campaign which convinced Stalin that Hitler was planning to finish off Britain before turning east – surely the most rational course of action for Germany, reasoned the Soviet dictator. Second, there seemed to be signs emanating from Berlin that Hitler wanted to renegotiate the Soviet-German relationship and maintain the non-aggression treaty, provided that Stalin was prepared to make political and territorial concessions. Stalin evidently thought that these 'peace' negotiations with Hitler would buy some more time. Third, Stalin was convinced that warnings about Barbarossa, even those from his own agents, were part of a British plot to provoke a war between Germany and the Soviet Union. Important to this belief was the mysterious flight of Hitler's deputy, Rudolph Hess, to Britain in May 1941. Hess was incarcerated and kept incommunicado by the British and Stalin suspected that some plot was afoot, including a possible attempt to switch the war around and line Britain and Germany up against the USSR. Finally, it may be that Stalin believed that it didn't really matter if the Germans surprised him with an attack. The real surprise of 22 June, after all, was that the Germans attacked with their entire main force immediately, without preliminary skirmishes and tactical battles on the frontier. No one on the Soviet side believed this was possible or likely until it actually happened. This final point goes to the heart of the recent reappraisal by historians of Stalin and 22 June 1941: he certainly bore the main responsibility for the disastrous impact of the surprise attack, but the responsibility was shared by the rest of the Soviet military-political leadership, including those generals who were later so keen to point the finger of blame exclusively at Stalin.

which functioned as a sort of war cabinet with main responsibility for the civilian aspects of the war effort. As Geoffrey Hosking comments: 'the Soviet leadership solved at an early stage a dilemma which Russia's First World War leaders had never coped with, the coordination of the civilian and military sides of government' (1990, p.274).

Under the *Stavka's* auspices there was a major overhaul of the Red Army's organisation and command structure in summer 1941. Of particular importance was the creation of Soviet equivalents to German Army Groups North, South and Centre. The Soviet equivalents were known as Fronts (or *Napravlenii* – directions). These were strategic commands that controlled a number of armies and which had responsibility for a major geographical sector of the front.

As Glantz comments: 'the fact that the Stavka was able to conceive of and execute so extensive a reorganisation at a time when the German advance placed them in a state of perpetual crisis-management was a tribute to the wisdom of the senior Red Army leadership.' (2001, p.64.)

Actually, organisational reform was a typical Soviet response to failure and crisis. Indeed, the Soviet regime had been in a state of perpetual crisis and emergency since its foundation in 1917. War, revolution, civil war, political upheaval, social and economic transformation, internal crises and external threats, war again – this had been the story of the Soviet state during its 20 or so years of existence. It would not have survived at all if it had not been able to do one thing effectively, if not efficiently; that was to mobilise its resources and energies in emergency situations. Perhaps the best example of this in 1941 was the dismantlement and evacuation of more than 1500 large-scale enterprises from European Russia to safety on the eastern side of the Ural Mountains. With the plant and machinery went hundreds of thousands of workers. Tens of thousands of trucks were used and up to a million and a half railway wagon loads of evacuation cargo. All of this took place under threat of rapidly advancing German forces and, often, under direct fire. As John Barber and Mark Harrison comment: 'the results of the industrial evacuation were of critical importance for the success of the Soviet war effort. It supplied the Red Army with the essential means of survival in the winter of 1941, without which nothing could have been done.' (1991, p.131.)

The other essential means of survival were human resources, particularly the reserves of people to replenish the armed forces. When the war began on the Eastern Front the Red Army was approximately five million strong with about 300 divisions. Most of this force had been wiped out by the end of 1941. However, the Soviets also had a civilian pool of 14 million with basic military training. On the outbreak of war more than five million reservists were called up and more were to follow. The result was that, despite massive casualties, the Red Army was eight million strong and had nearly 600 divisions by the end of December 1941.

Underestimation of the Red Army's reserves and the Soviet capacity for human and material mobilisation was among the Germans' biggest mistakes. If the *Blitzkrieg* was to succeed, it had to succeed quickly, before Soviet reserves were mobilised and deployed to swing the balance of military power on the front-line decisively against the *Wehrmacht*.

The Germans' best chance of success in 1941 was to win the battle for Moscow. The fall or encirclement of the Soviet capital would have been a devastating military, political and psychological blow. It is doubtful whether Stalin and the Soviet regime would have been able to survive defeat at Moscow.

On the Soviet side the key to the successful defence of Moscow was threefold. First, and most obvious, was the availability of just enough reserves of men and matériel to block the advance of the Germans' Operation Typhoon. In mid-November Moscow was defended by a quarter of a million troops with 1250 artillery guns, 500 tanks and 600–700 aircraft, and was vastly outnumbered by the Germans. But by early December the Soviet force had grown to over a million, the defence of Moscow was secure and the Red Army was ready to counter-attack. Among the reinforcements were divisions transferred from the USSR's far eastern borders – a redeployment authorised by Stalin when he became convinced by his agents in Tokyo that Japan was intent on attacking the United States, not the Soviet Union. Among the reinforcing units were many Siberians, a group destined to play a crucial role in the defence of Stalingrad in 1942.

Second, there was Stalin's appointment of General Georgii K. Zhukov as Commander-in-Chief of the defence of the city. Zhukov was the greatest Soviet commander of the war. He was tough, disciplined, and determined, as well as bruising and brutal in his handling of operational matters. He was coarse and not one to suffer fools gladly. Dauntless in battle, he was one of the few Soviet generals prepared also to stand up to Stalin. When war broke out he was Chief of the General Staff, but was subsequently transferred to frontline duties. In September 1941 Zhukov was sent to Leningrad to organise its defence. By this time the city was besieged by German and Finnish forces (seeking revenge for the Winter War) and virtually cut off from the rest of the country. On 22 September Hitler issued a directive that he had 'decided to erase the city ... from the face of the earth. I have no interest in the further existence of this large city after the defeat of Soviet Russia.' The Germans never did take Leningrad, but more than a million civilians died during the course of a 900-day siege from 1941 to 1944. In October 1941 Stalin recalled Zhukov to Moscow, another city Hitler intended to raze to the ground, if he could lay his hands on it. Not only did Zhukov mobilise and maintain a successful defence; he also masterminded a counter-offensive in front of Moscow that was the Germans' first big defeat in the whole war.

Third, there was Stalin's own role in holding the line at Moscow. As the Germans approached Moscow in October there was panic in the city following preparations and rumours concerning an evacuation. Indeed, some government ministries and officials were evacuated to east of the Urals. But Stalin stayed in Moscow and his continuing presence helped steady the population's nerve. On 17 October it was announced by Radio Moscow that Stalin was staying in the city. On 6 and again on 7 November Stalin appeared in public and spoke on the anniversary of the Bolshevik seizure of power in Russia. His message was patriotic rather than communist, the tone confident but not triumphalistic, and the two speeches were replete with references to great Russian defences of the motherland in the past. On 7 November Stalin told members of the armed forces parading through Red Square on their way to the front:

'The whole world is looking to you as the force capable of destroying the plundering hordes of the German invaders. The enslaved peoples of Europe ... look to you as their liberators. A great liberation mission has fallen to your lot. Be worthy of this mission! The war you are waging is a war of liberation, a just war. Let the manly images of our great ancestors – Alexander Nevsky [who defeated the Swedes], Dimitry Donskoy [who beat the Tartars], Kurma Minin and Dimitry Pozharsky [who drove the Poles out of Moscow], Alexander Suvorov and Mikhail Kutuzov [the Russian hero generals of the Napoleonic wars] – inspire you in this war. May the victorious banner of the great Lenin be your lodestar.'

(Stalin, 1943, p.23)

This intervention by Stalin came at a critical moment of the German threat to Moscow and was an important psychological turning-point in the defence of the city. Not that Stalin himself was incapable of feeling the strain. When the Germans began their final advance to Moscow in October 1941 the Soviet dictator lapsed into the third person and told General Ivan Konev: 'Comrade Stalin is not a traitor. Comrade Stalin is an honest person. Comrade Stalin will do everything to correct the situation that has been created.'

On the German side, the reasons for their failure to take

Moscow were multiple, too. When Army Group Centre reached Moscow its supply lines were stretched and it had lost much of its mobility. The Germans had also suffered substantial casualties. By the time of Operation Typhoon, German losses on the Eastern Front were in the order of three-quarters of a million – about 25 per cent of their original attack force. There were commensurate losses of tanks, vehicles and other equipment. In addition, the German advance on Moscow had been slowed down by the weather, first the autumn mud and then the snow and ice of the bitter Russian winter. German troops were suffering badly from the wintry conditions, although the weather was indiscriminate in its effects. Quite simply, the German *Blitzkrieg* had run out of momentum, and faced with a staunch defence by Zhukov's increasingly replenished forces, only a precipitate Soviet collapse could have taken the *Wehrmacht* all the way into or even around Moscow.

After the war many of the surviving German generals argued that Moscow could have been taken had Hitler stuck with the *Wehrmacht's* original priority of destroying the Red Army in front of Moscow in a decisive battle of annihilation. But in late July, so the argument goes, Hitler paused Army Group Centre's advance towards Moscow and redirected forces to the north to attack Leningrad and to Army Group South's operations in the Ukraine. In the south the Germans had encountered strong Soviet opposition. It was in the southern theatre that much of Soviet armour was concentrated, a priority which reflected Stalin's belief that this would be the primary direction of the German invasion.

Hitler's decision to assert the priority of the southern theatre reflected his obsession with gaining control of the vast economic resources of the Ukraine and the Caucasus. As he told his adjutant on 28 July 1941: 'though Moscow was also a big industrial centre, the south was even more important, with oil, grain, absolutely everything that was necessary to secure living-space. A land flowing with milk and honey.' (Boog *et al.*, 1998, p.1096.)

Both at the time, and after the war, some *Wehrmacht* generals argued that Hitler's redirection of the attack dissipated German forces and allowed the Russians time to regroup, draw upon their reserves and mount an effective defence of Moscow. At the same time, the momentum and timing of the German advance were being lost and it was destined to run into weather problems if the Russians weren't finished off before the autumn rains.

As in the case of similar discussions about Hitler's strategic and tactical mistakes in relation to Stalingrad, a closer look at the position reveals a more complex picture than the self-serving arguments of German generals re-fighting the Second World War in their fantasies. Hitler's decision to redirect the German attack had sound military, as well as economic, motives. In July 1941 the *Wehrmacht* ran into strong Soviet counter-attacks in the Smolensk area, which held up the German advance for several weeks. In prospect was further hard fighting along the road to Moscow. Moreover, there were substantial enemy forces to the north and south of Army Group Centre and these threatened the flanks of any German advance to Moscow. But having dealt devastating blows to

Soviet forces in both the northern and southern theatres, the Germans resumed offensive action in the central sector in September. According to David Glantz (2001, p.213), this was the best time to do so, since an earlier march on Moscow by the *Wehrmacht* would have faced far stronger Red Army opposition, not least from the several armies of the Soviet South-western Front that the Germans had attacked and destroyed in August as a result of Hitler's redirection of the campaign.

Although the Germans failed to take Moscow, Army Group South's successful conquest of the Ukraine created a platform for a campaign directed against Stalingrad and the Caucasus in 1942. Arguably, Operation Barbarossa failed at Smolensk in July–August 1941. The Soviets lost the battle for Smolensk and suffered heavy casualties, but they bought some valuable time to prepare their defences further east and to mobilise their resources and reserves.

As early as summer 1941 the war on the Eastern Front had become a battle of attrition. Although he still hoped for total victory in 1941, Hitler saw more clearly than his generals that the character of the war had changed fundamentally. The control of resources would now determine its outcome, not the generals' fantasy of a *Vernichtungschlacht* – a decisive annihilatory battle in front of Moscow. Hitler's perception of this reality was sharpened by the American entry into the war in December 1941, following the Japanese attack at Pearl Harbour and Germany's supporting declaration of war on the United States. In June 1941 the USSR and Britain had allied together; now there came into being a grand Anglo-Soviet-

American coalition, whose first priority was to defeat Germany. The European war had become a world war and Hitler was locked into a global battle for survival against the Allied coalition.

Germany's best chance of survival, and of winning, if not the war, then a war-winning position, was to secure the means to continue indefinitely a global battle of attrition. That chance was to come at Stalingrad in 1942.

chapter three

HITLER'S QUEST FOR OIL:

the road to Stalingrad,
April – August 1942

For 1942 Hitler planned another *Blitzkrieg* campaign in Russia. However, its scope, aims and overall goals were very different from those of Operation Barbarossa. For a start the German army was incapable of a strategic offensive across the whole of the Eastern Front. Despite its great victories, the *Wehrmacht* had taken a severe battering at the hands of the Russians in 1941–2. By March 1942 the Germans had suffered casualties of 1.1 million dead, wounded, missing or captured, some 35 per cent of their Eastern army's strength. Only eight out of 162 divisions were at full strength and operational capacity. Some 625,000 replacements were needed to bring the Eastern army back up to scratch. The army's mobility was severely impaired by the loss of 40,000 lorries, 40,000 motorcycles and nearly 30,000 cars, not to speak of thousands of tanks. Of the 180,000 draught animals (mainly horses) also lost as a result of enemy action, only 20,000 had been replaced by March 1942.

The only realistic option was an offensive on a single front. Hitler's attention focused on the southern front and on the quest for oil. In the Transcaucasus, the area deep in the south of the USSR centred on the Caucasus mountains, were the oil fields that supplied 90 per cent of Soviet fuel. Hitler had both short- and long-term motives for wanting to seize these oil fields. Denying the Russians their oil was one short-term aim; another was the desperate need to increase oil supplies to Germany and its Axis allies.

In the longer term, Hitler needed the means to fight a prolonged war of attrition against the Allies on a multiplicity of fronts. A long war was clearly the only prospect in Russia, and

Hitler worried increasingly about the implications of the entry of the United States into the conflict. American economic and military power had been crucial in swinging the balance against Germany during the First World War. He was particularly concerned about the danger to his *Festung Europa* (Fortress Europe) of an Anglo-American invasion of France. Although that invasion did not take place until June 1944, in mid-1942 it seemed a matter of months rather than years away. German predominance, if not outright victory, had to be established on the Eastern Front before the Allied invasion of France. In that event Germany would be faced with the prospect of a two-front land war in Europe, which it would inevitably lose. This was the background to Chief-of-Staff Halder's statements in March 1942 that the 'war will be decided in the east' and 'only through the possession of that territory [Transcaucasia] will the German war empire be viable in the long-term' (Boog et al, 2001, pp.844, 860). Hitler agreed. In June 1942 he told his generals 'if we don't get to Maykop and Groznyy [Soviet oil cities in Transcaucasia], I shall have to pack up ("liquidieren") the war' (Goerlitz, 1963, p.155).

A thrust to the Caucasus offered other economic advantages. If the Germans did succeed in occupying Transcaucasia, including the Azerbaijan oil capital of Baku, an important Allied supply route to Russia would be cut. Anglo-American supplies shipped via the Persian Gulf would be forced to make a huge detour through Kazakhstan in the Soviet central Asia. A German advance south would involve occupation of the Donets Basin (the Donbas) – the mineral-rich industrial heartland of the Ukraine – and conquest of the fertile lands of the Don and Kuban rivers. Again, denial of these resources to the Russians loomed large in Hitler's calculations.

Finally, Hitler was anxious about the security of the Rumanian oil fields in Ploesti – the main supplier of the German war machine. These oil fields had been attacked a number of times by Soviet bombers. Damage was light but the potential for a destructive air campaign was clear. 'Now in the era of air power', Hitler had said in January 1941, 'Russia can turn the Rumanian oil fields into an expanse of smoking debris ... and the very life of the Axis depends on those fields.'

The deceptively simple goals of the German summer campaign of 1942 were set out in Führer Directive No.41, dated 5 April 1942:

> 'all available forces will be concentrated on the main operations in the Southern sector, with the aim of destroying the enemy before the Don, in order to secure the Caucasian oil fields and the passes through the Caucasian mountains themselves.'
> (Trevor-Roper, 1964, p.117)

The priority attached to the seizure of critical resources was very much Hitler's own; it was a return, indeed, to his economic-military ambitions of the previous summer. In August 1941 when the German high command were debating how to finish Russia off Hitler had issued a directive stating that 'the most important aim to be achieved before the onset of winter is not the capture of Moscow but, rather, the occupation of the Crimea, of the industrial and coal-mining area of the

Donets Basin, the cutting of the Russian supply routes from the Caucasus oil fields . . .' (Hayward, 1998, p.9). As late as December 1941 Hitler had still hoped for a German advance all the way to the Volga and to Baku.

However, unlike 1941, Hitler did not necessarily expect to win the war in the east in 1942. The aim was to deal the Red Army a devastating blow by destroying their forces in the Don and the Donbas areas and to secure an economic stranglehold on oil and other Soviet resources. But neither Hitler nor his generals expected complete victory in the war, or even on the Eastern Front. This was a campaign designed to acquire the means and the position to continue the global war over the long term. As General Douglas McArthur later said, at stake in the Stalingrad campaign was Germany's ability to wage war against the Soviet-Western alliance for another 10 years.

Post-war claims notwithstanding, at the time most of the German military leadership shared Hitler's strategic concept, or at least offered no realistic alternative to it. The German generals' main concern, however, was not the prize of oil but the defeat and destruction of the Red Army. This operational priority was reflected in Directive No. 41 and in detailed planning for the campaign. The basic plan was to occupy the Donets Basin and all the territory west of the Don. Soviet forces in these areas would be encircled and destroyed and a defensive line established along the Don itself. When that was achieved the main German force would cross the Don south of Rostov and head for the Kuban and the Caucasus (see Map 3, p.xxi).

Significantly, the capture of Stalingrad was not a prime goal of the initial plan of campaign. 'At the start Stalingrad was no more than a name on a map', claimed one German General (Liddell Hart, 1948, p.199). But, as Directive No. 41 stated: 'every effort will be made to reach Stalingrad itself, or at least bring the city under fire from heavy artillery so that it may no longer be of any use as an industrial or communications centre.' (Trevor-Roper, 1964, p.119.)

Stalingrad was located on the bend of the Volga that brought that river to within 50 miles of the most easterly point of the bend in the Don. From the point of view of defending the line of the Don, it made sense for the Germans to occupy key points on the western bank of the Volga in the vicinity of Stalingrad. This would enable the construction of a defensive landbridge between the two rivers. Bringing Stalingrad under fire would also halt the flow of oil up the Volga to central and northern Russia.

'Operation Blau' (Blue) was the codename for the German campaign. Charged with its implementation was Army Group South, commanded by Field Marshal Fedor von Bock. Shortly after Blau's launch, Army Group South was divided into two groups: Army Group A (1st Panzer Army and 17th Army) and Army Group B (6th Army and 4th Panzer Army). In addition there was the 11th Army located in the Crimea. Supporting the German armies were a large number of Rumanian, Italian and Hungarian divisions. One solution to the manpower shortage problem had been to secure an increase in the military commitment of Germany's Axis allies – a solution sought very actively by Berlin in early 1942. By the time of the battle of Stalingrad there were 24 Rumanian, ten Italian and ten Hungarian divisions serving on the Russian front. Most of these divisions formed part of Axis contingents on the Don front – the Hungarian 2nd, Italian 8th and the Rumanian 3rd and 4th armies. German reliance on such a large measure of support from its Axis allies was to have fatal consequences.

The two million strong German and Axis force consisted of 89 divisions including nine armoured divisions. By far its strongest element was what became Army Group B, which had 50 of the divisions. Its task was to strike east from the Kursk and Karkhov regions in the direction of Voronezh and then south-east towards the great bend of the Don River. The battle having been won in Don country, the Hungarian, Italian and Rumanian armies would then be deployed defensively along the river while German divisions turned south to join in Army Group A's drive for the Caucasus.

Before the start of the main campaign the Germans deemed some preliminary operations necessary. The first of these was a campaign in the south to complete the conquest of the Crimea. This involved retaking control of the Kerch Peninsula and wresting control of the city-fortress of Sevastopol, the last Soviet outpost in the Crimea proper. Tasked with this campaign was General Eric von Manstein's 11th Army which, on completion of the operation, would then cross the Kerch strait to the mainland and join in the march to the Caucasus (see Map 3, pxxi).

The Germans' Kerch offensive began on 8 May and within a

fortnight it had resulted in the destruction of three Soviet armies with a total of 21 divisions. Many Soviet soldiers were able to escape across the Kerch strait to the mainland, but the Germans nevertheless took 170,000 prisoners. Von Manstein next turned his attention to Sevastopol. The assault began on 2 June with a massive aerial and artillery bombardment. During the course of a month-long siege the *Luftwaffe* flew more than 23,000 sorties and dropped 20,000 tons of bombs on the city. The Germans also shipped in their very heaviest artillery, including guns which fired one ton, 1.5-ton and, even seven-ton shells. A Soviet eyewitness reported:

> 'About 2,000 guns and mortars kept firing at our positions without a moment's interval. Shells whined overhead and exploded on all sides. The thunder of guns merged into a deafening roar, splitting our eardrums ... German aircraft were in the air above our positions all day long. We could not hear their engines in the continuous thunder of guns and shell explosions ... A whirlwind of fire was raging at all our positions. The sky was clouded by smoke from thousands of bombs and shells ... An enormous dark grey cloud of smoke and dust rose higher and higher and finally eclipsed the sun.' (Hayward, 1998, pp.96–7)

Following infantry and amphibious assaults Sevastopol fell in early July. Soviet fatalities were in the tens of thousands and the Germans took 95,000 more prisoners. But the Crimean mop-up operation had taken longer and cost more than expected. The Germans suffered 75,000 casualties, including 25,000 dead. The Soviets had lost badly but the defenders of Sevastopol had put up an awesome defence that prefigured what the Germans were to face at Stalingrad.

As a reward for his success Hitler promoted Manstein to Field Marshal. He was then transferred to the northern theatre of operations to take part in the siege of Leningrad. It was a sign of Hitler's confidence that to go with Manstein were many divisions and units of the 11th Army that could otherwise have been tasked to cross the Kerch strait and head for the Caucasus.

Meanwhile, the action was also underway in the Donbas – the mineral rich basin of the Ukraine. Its initiation, however, had come from an unexpected quarter. On 12 May the Soviets launched a major offensive designed to retake the city of Kharkov – second city of the Ukraine, fourth largest in the USSR, and an important centre of industry, communications and transport. Unfortunately, the Soviet offensive coincided with German plans for offensive action in the same area preparatory to the launch of Operation Blau. The German 6th Army and 1st Panzer Army were already concentrating and mobilising and were able to mount an effective defence and counter-offensive. Not only did the Russians fail to recapture Kharkov, but the three Soviet armies involved in the operation were encircled by the Germans and largely destroyed. Soviet casualties were nearly 280,000, including 170,000 killed, missing, or captured. Around 650 tanks were lost and nearly 5000 artillery pieces. The battle was over by 28 May. General Ewald von Kleist, commander of 1st Panzer, surveyed the carnage around Kharkov:

> 'The fierceness of the fighting is testified by the battlefield: at focal points the ground as far as one can see is so thickly covered with the cadavers of men and horses that it is difficult to find a passage for one's command car.' (Boog et al, 2001, p.950)

To an extent the Soviets were unlucky to run into such strong German forces, which just happened to be nearly ready and waiting for them. Moreover, as Geoffrey Jukes has commented (Jukes, 1968, pp.15–16), had Bock launched his attacks in the Kharkov area first then Army Group South might have run unexpectedly into strong Soviet forces and found itself in serious trouble.

But the Soviet disaster at Kharkov also stemmed from Moscow's own misconceptions and miscalculations. While the Germans were preparing Operation Blau the Soviets were making their own plans. The basic strategic approach of Stalin and the Soviet high command was that for 1942 the Red Army would stay mainly on the defensive. At the same time some localised offensive actions were agreed, the largest of these operations being the one at Kharkov. Stalin certainly favoured this offensive but it seems that the initiative and pressure for action came mainly from Marshal Semyon Timoshenko and other officers of the Red Army's South Western Front that conducted the operation. (Timoshenko was subsequently transferred to other duties in the Northern theatre of operations).

At the same time the impetus for Soviet offensive action at Kharkov needs to be seen in the context of a larger strategic miscalculation. Like the Germans, the Soviets had underestimated their enemy. Stalin and the *Stavka* believed that in the winter of 1941–2 they had come close to precipitating German military collapse on the Eastern Front and that German reserves and resources were exhausted. A further misapprehension was the belief that the main German threat was to the central sector of the Eastern Front and that any major offensive action would be directed at Moscow. The root of this misperception – which persisted throughout the Stalingrad campaign – was threefold. First, was Stalin's belief that, as in 1941, the decisive struggle would be fought before Moscow which was deemed more important strategically and psychologically than any other Soviet target. Second, there was the fact that 70 German divisions remained concentrated in the central sector, many only 100 miles from Moscow. Third, was the impact of a very effective deception campaign mounted by the Germans – Operation Kreml. This consisted of extensive fake preparations for an attack on Moscow, helping to persuade Stalin that Operation Blau, even once it was well underway, was a diversion or, at most, an operation of secondary importance.

In the context of this web of speculation and calculation the campaign to retake Kharkov did not seem such a great risk, particularly given the large Soviet force committed to the operation – three-quarters of a million strong, including many of the newly-organised tank brigades, the Red Army's armoured counter to the German panzer divisions.

Although the Kharkov operation was very costly for the Soviets, important lessons were learned too: above all, the wisdom of staying on the strategic defensive and the necessity for retreat in adverse circumstances. For the Germans, on the other hand, the Kharkov victory inflated their expectations of success in the southern campaign and reinforced their belief in Soviet weakness.

Operation Blau was launched on 28 June 1942. Or, rather, an operation called 'Braunschweig' began because the Germans had changed the codename following the so-called 'Reichel affair'. Major Joachim Reichel, operations officer for the 23rd Panzer division, was carrying the plans for Blau when his plane crashed on 19 June. The plans fell into enemy hands and the Germans hastened to start the operation before the Soviets could prepare their defences. They needn't have worried. Stalin was still convinced that the main German attack would be launched at Moscow and believed that the plans for Operation Blau were an intelligence plant of a false operation. By mid-July, however, he was beginning to revise this assessment. It was becoming clear that the German southern offensive was an operation of major proportions.

Alan Clarke has provided this evocative image of the German advance across the southern Russian steppes in summer 1942:

> 'The progress of the German columns could be discerned at thirty or forty miles' distance. An enormous dust cloud towered in the sky, thickened by smoke from burning villages and gunfire. Heavy and dark at the head of the column, the smoke lingered in the still atmosphere of the summer long after the tanks had passed on, a hanging barrage of brown haze stretching back to the western horizon.' (1965, p.205)

Like all major military operations Blau (as we shall continue to call it) was a messy, chaotic and often haphazard campaign. There were advances and retreats, victories and defeats, triumphs and tragedies. Numerous crises had to be dealt with, and important command decisions were taken at all levels. Forces were disposed, manoeuvred and committed by both sides. Objectives had to be fought for, battles, both big and small, waged and won. Outcomes were mostly predictable but far from certain. Nevertheless, as the map shows (see Map 4, p.xxii) throughout July and August there was a clear pattern of rapid German advances and successes. By the end of July the Germans occupied the whole of the Donets Basin, much of Don country and were heading towards Stalingrad and the Caucasus.

As in summer 1941 the German high command was dizzy with success. On 6 July Halder stated: 'we have overestimated the enemy's strength and the offensive has completely smashed him up.' On 20 July Hitler told Halder: 'The Russian is finished'. Halder replied: 'I must admit that it looks that way'. By the end of August the Germans were on the Volga and Stalingrad was under siege. In the south they had reached the foothills of the Caucasus, Maikop had been seized, the oil fields of Grozny in Chechnya were under threat, and the Germans were poised to occupy the entire east coast of the Black Sea and to march on Baku. On 21 August 1942 the German flag was raised atop Mount Elbruz, the highest peak of the Caucasus. This was the moment of the maximum extent of German penetration in to the USSR during the Second World War. In population and resource terms almost half the Soviet Union was under German occupation.

During July and August the Germans took 625,000 Soviet prisoners and captured or destroyed 7000 tanks, 6000 artillery pieces and more than 400 aircraft. German casualties were high too; some 200,000 in August alone. Soviet losses were significant, particularly when totalled with those at Kharkov and in the Crimea, but even then were nothing compared to the scale of the millions in summer 1941. The reason for the contrast was simple: the Soviets were withdrawing rather than standing and fighting as in 1941. The general order for strategic retreat was issued by the *Stavka* on 6 July. This meant that while the Germans were successful in occupying territory they were not achieving their other strategic goal of encircling and destroying enemy forces – at least not on a sufficiently large scale. As Ziemke and Bauer point out (Ziemke and Bauer 1987, pp.343–4, 510–12) the problem with operations based on deep penetration and large-scale envelopment of enemy forces is that they require the opponent to stand and fight rather than attempt to evade encirclement.

Of course, an alternative interpretation of the situation in summer 1942 was that the Soviet enemy was weak and in full-scale retreat, and this explained the relatively small number of prisoners taken. This was the prevalent view on the German side. Its impact on Hitler himself can be seen in the crucial strategic reorientation of Operation Blau that occurred during the course of July 1942.

In its original conception Blau was a unified and co-ordinated operation in which the goals of Army Group South as a whole would be achieved on a phased basis. First would come control of the Don and the Volga, to be followed by a major push south to the Caucasus. On 9 July, however, Army Group South was split into the separate commands of Army Groups A and B. Bock took charge of Army Group B while Army Group A was headed by Field Marshal Wilhelm List. Then, on 13 July, Hitler dismissed Bock following a dispute about the capture of the Soviet city of Voronezh (he was replaced by Field Marshal Baron von Weichs). That same day 4th Panzer Army was directed by Hitler to join in Army Group A's (1st Panzer and 17th Army) advance south to Rostov-on-Don, an important staging post on the road to the Caucasus. On 17 July Hitler indicated that his intention was to destroy the Soviet armies between the Don and the Donets in front of Rostov, while at the same time reaching the Volga south of Stalingrad.

On 23 July Hitler issued Führer Directive No.45. This stated that 'in a campaign which has lasted little more than three weeks, the broad objectives outlined by me for the southern flank of the Eastern front have been largely achieved.' Army Group A was now tasked to destroy the enemy south of Rostov and then 'to occupy the entire Eastern coastline of the Black Sea'. Supported by 11th Army divisions crossing the Kerch strait from the Crimea, Army Group A would also take Maikop, Grozny and Baku in an operation codenamed 'Edelweiss'. Army Group B – in effect, the 6th Army plus back up support from Axis divisions – was directed to 'thrust forward to Stalingrad, to smash the enemy forces concentrated there, to occupy the town, and to block the land communications between the Don and the Volga.' (Trevor-Roper, 1964, pp.129–30.)

By common consent Hitler's new directive was his fatal mistake that summer of 1942. Directive No. 45 was important for two reasons. Operation Blau had been reoriented southward, indeed seems to have been temporarily eclipsed by the projected Edelweiss operation. More important, the summer offensive had been split and would now pursue two strategic goals simultaneously: the capture of the Caucasian oilfields and the occupation of Stalingrad. But the Germans were not strong enough to achieve both goals at the same time. It is doubtful that they could have succeeded quickly in the Caucasus in any event, short of complete Russian collapse, as distance, logistics and terrain were against them. On the other hand, they might have taken Stalingrad had they concentrated quickly enough on that goal. As it was the 6th Army was neither strong enough nor mobile enough (fuel and transport were in short supply because of the priority given to Edelweiss) to reach Stalingrad before the Soviets had time to build up their defences and to transfer reserves that had been held back for the defence of Moscow.

Rostov had first been occupied, temporarily it turned out, by the Germans in November 1941. On 23–24 July 1942 the Germans recaptured the 'gateway to the Caucasus'. On 1 August most of 4th Panzer Army was re-attached to Army Group B and redirected to attack Stalingrad from the south, but crucial time and momentum had been lost. At the end of July, General Alfred Jodl, operations chief of the German armed forces high command, noted that 'the fate of the Caucasus will be decided at Stalingrad'. Stalingrad was the pivot of the defensive block on the Don and Volga that the Germans needed to establish quickly in order to protect their drive to the Caucasus from a flanking Soviet counter-attack.

Hitler's directive on 23 July to take Stalingrad reflected his overweening confidence. But the redeployment of the 4th

Panzer Army to attack the city together with 6th Army was recognition by the Germans that perhaps it wouldn't be so easy. Once this commitment to take Stalingrad by a dual attack was made there was no turning back. Whatever the arguments about the military necessity of occupying the city itself, as opposed to simply bringing it under fire and controlling the Volga, politically and psychologically the capture of Stalingrad became absolutely essential. Failure to do so would be a significant defeat that would impact greatly on German morale, undermine the Axis alliance, and provide a major boost to the Soviets and their western allies. These issues Hitler understood much better than his generals.

By mid-July the Soviets were beginning to realise the seriousness of the German threat and the growing importance of the defence of Stalingrad. On 12 July Stalin established the Stalingrad Front, a force of 38 divisions (20 of which were below strength, however), consisting mainly of three reserve armies – the 62nd, 63rd and 64th Soviet Armies. On 19 July Stalingrad itself was put on an immediate war footing. At the end of July *Stavka* released more divisions from its reserves and mounted counter-attacks on Stalingrad's flanks and on the approaches to the city to relieve the pressure of the German advance.

In mid-August Winston Churchill went to Moscow to meet Stalin. The Soviet leader told him that:

> 'the Germans were making a tremendous effort to get to Baku and Stalingrad. He did not know how they had been able to get together so many troops and tanks, and so many Hungarian,

Italian and Rumanian divisions. He was sure that they had drained the whole of Europe for troops. In Moscow the position was sound, but he could not guarantee in advance that the Russians would be able to withstand a German attack. In the south they had been unable to stop the German offensive.'

Throughout August the defences of Stalingrad were readied for siege. But perhaps as important to the final outcome as military measures was the Soviet political mobilisation to rally the whole country against the German attack.

Among the more memorable passages in Alexander Werth's classic *Russia at War* (1964, pp.372–94) is his description of the emotional *patrie-en-danger* atmosphere in Russia that 'Black Summer' as the Germans swiftly advanced south. 'Throughout the summer of 1942, the feeling that Russia – Holy Russia – was again in mortal danger grew from day to day.' The crisis atmosphere reached fever pitch with the fall of Rostov towards the end of July. The first in a series of essentially political responses to the crisis came on 28 July with the issue by Stalin of Order No.227, familiarly known as 'Not a step back!' (*Ni shagu nazad!*). Order No.227 was a dec-laration-cum-directive signed by Stalin in his capacity as People's Commissar of Defence. Unlike other orders it was not published but was instead read out to the armed forces. All officers were required to sign a declaration that they had read and understood the order. (A full English translation of the order is appended at pp.203–10 below).

Order No.227 frankly set out the grave situation facing the Soviet Union and called on the armed forces to do their patriotic duty. Its rallying call was: 'Not a step back! This must now be our chief slogan. It is necessary to defend to the last drop of blood every position, every metre of Soviet territory, to cling on to every shred of Soviet earth and defend it to the utmost.'

Orders for no retreat were not novel. Soviet soldiers were forbidden by Red Army regulations from surrendering and allowing themselves to be taken prisoner. In summer 1941, as the number of Soviet soldiers surrendering swelled into the millions, Stalin authorised a series of draconian directives threatening dire punishment for 'deserters' and 'cowards'. The best known, but little understood, of these is Order No.270 of 16 August 1941 which contrasted the heroic actions of Red Army units which on when encircled by the Germans with those 'cowardly' officers and men that gave themselves up without a fight. The order threatened that 'commanders and political workers who tore off their insignia during battle and deserted to the rear or surrendered to enemy captivity will be considered deliberate deserters whose families will be liable to arrest as relatives of those violating their oath to their country.' Further, that the families of non-commissioned ranks who did not fight to the end would lose state benefits and assistance. (A translation of the full text of this order is appended to this book at pp.197–202).

The context and meaning of Order No.227 was somewhat different. In effect, it was a call for a disciplined, orderly retreat and for last redoubt sacrifices when necessary. Its aim was to control the strategic withdrawal of Soviet forces while at the same time psychologically preparing the troops to make a final stand at Stalingrad and elsewhere.

Geoffrey Jukes compares the Stalin order with Churchill's 'blood, toil, tears, and sweat' speech of May 1940 which helped rally the British people at a time of great national danger as the *Wehrmacht* was beginning its triumphant march through western Europe towards the English Channel (1985, p.233). Another comparison would be with what Richard Overy calls the 'moral moment' of the Battle of Britain – 'when the uncertainties and divisions ... gave way to a greater sense of purpose and a more unified people'. (2000, p.120.) The order was the beginning of the moral moment that was the Battle of Stalingrad.

Accounts of the effect of Order No.227 on the Soviet armed forces are mixed, but the balance of the reports suggest that it was inspirational, a major boost to morale and moral courage at a time when things seemed to be once again falling apart. At the same time, the order also contained various provisions for the establishment of 'punishment battalions' for officers guilty of cowardice, indiscipline or insufficient resolve who would redeem themselves (whether they wanted to or not!) by being given the most dangerous assignments. Instructions were also issued on the establishment of detachments behind front-line forces that would shoot deserters, panickers and unauthorised retreaters. These instructions were probably the reason the order was not published – to do so would have handed the enemy a propaganda coup. However, again there was nothing new about such orders, which had been issued and implemented since summer 1941. Moreover, such a harsh disciplinary regime was not unusual in the Soviet context and it reflected the gravity of the crisis facing the regime as the Germans advanced to Stalingrad. But the detailing and statement of sanctions against 'waverers' was significant, not so much because it encouraged discipline, but because it bolstered those who were inclined to heroism. In this life and death struggle there would be no quarter or concession to those tempted to give up the fight.

Draconian discipline was also deemed necessary by the authorities because of the make-up of the Soviet army. Most were new recruits and conscripts, the Soviets having lost half their strength as a result of the Barbarossa *Blitzkrieg*. There were some elite formations, but many of the massed infantry divisions had been only hurriedly and partially trained. The only way of maintaining order under fire, it seemed, was the threat of the harshest discipline and punishment. As Alan Clarke noted: 'these conditions – the long withdrawal across a burning homeland – are the most difficult in which to preserve morale, particularly among a relatively primitive and imperfectly trained body, as the bulk of the Red Army units were at this time' (1965, p.213). The Soviet solution to this problem was patriotic political mobilisation, on the one hand, and peremptory punishment, on the other.

The second strand of Soviet political mobilisation that summer was anti-German hate propaganda. On 19 July the Soviet army newspaper *Red Star* (*Krasnaya Zvezda*) published Konstantin Simonov's poem 'Kill Him':

'If your home is dear to you, where your Russian mother nursed you . . .
If your mother is dear to you, and you cannot bear the thought of the German slapping her wrinkled face;

If your father's memory is dear to you; if you do not want him to turn in his grave;

If you do not want the German to tear down his picture, with the Crosses he earned in the last war, and stamp on it:

If you do not want your old teacher to be hanged outside the old school-house;

If you do not want her, whom for so long you did not even dare kiss, to be stretched out naked on the floor so that, amid hatred, cries and tears, three German curs should take what belongs to your manly love;

If you do not want to give away all that you call your country, then kill a German, kill a German every time you see one.

And if your brother has killed a German, then he not you, is the soldier;

Kill a German, so that he, and not you, should lie in the ground,

Kill him, so that the tears should flow in his home, not yours;

Let his house burn, not yours; let his wife, and not yours, be a widow;

Let his mother weep, and not yours; let his family and not yours wait in vain.

Kill him, kill him every time you see him.' (Werth, 1946, p.133)

This was a far cry from 'Wait for Me', Simonov's tragic lament in autumn 1941 for the missing millions of Red Army soldiers:

'Wait for me, and I'll return, only wait very hard.

Wait, when you are filled with sorrow as you watch the yellow rain;

Wait, when the winds sweep the snowdrifts,
Wait in the sweltering heat.
Wait when others have stopped waiting ...
Wait, for I'll return, defying every death.
And let those who did not wait say that I was lucky;
They will never understand that in the midst of death,
You, with your waiting, saved me ...' (Werth, 1964, pp.260–1)

Since the publication of that poem more and more evidence of German atrocities and massacres on a massive scale had come to light. In the summer of 1942 it seemed that the only choice was to exterminate or be exterminated. This was the theme of another famous piece of hate propaganda, published by *Red Star* on 13 August 1942. Ilya Ehrenburg's brutal but elegiac article 'Kill the Germans':

'Every day brings us new ordeals. Russia's heart is bleeding. The enemy is trampling underfoot the rich fields of the Kuban. He can already smell the oil of the Caucasus ... There are green forests on the map of Russia, blue rivers and brown mountains. Now the map seems drenched in blood. The country is crying in its agony: "Cleanse me of the Germans!". One can bear anything: the plague, and hunger and death. But one cannot bear the Germans. One cannot bear these fish-eyed oafs contemptuously snorting at everything Russian, as they come over the Russian land from the Carpathians to the Caucasus. We cannot live as long as these grey-green slugs are alive ... Today there are no books; today there are no stars in the sky; today there is only one thought: Kill the Germans. Kill them all and dig them into the earth. Then we can go to sleep. Then we can think again of life, and books, and girls, and happiness. But now we must fight like madmen, live like fanatics ... The German is the screen standing between us and life. We want to live. And, in order to live, we must kill Germans ... Everybody knows we shall kill them all. But we must do it quickly; or they will desecrate the whole of Russia and torture to death millions more people.' (Werth, 1946, pp.170–1)

Although such outbursts were sponsored and supported by the Soviet regime, writers such as Ehrenburg and Simonov needed no prompting. The hate came from the heart. Anti-German feelings were spontaneous and widespread throughout Soviet society. Hardly surprising in the circumstances, but important for our understanding of the depth of Russian resistance to the Germans in their hour of mortal national danger.

A third feature of Soviet political mobilisation in summer 1942 was the 'nationalisation' and professionalisation of the armed forces. When the Germans attacked in 1941 Stalin's initial response was to strengthen Communist Party political control over the armed forces at every level. But, as the battle for Stalingrad took shape, developments in party-army relations took a different turn. The press was filled with articles on the importance of professionalism and technical ability rather than ideological dogma. Officers, in particular, were singled out as having a special patriotic duty in the defence of the country. At the end of July new decorations were introduced for officers only: the Orders of Kutuzov, Nevsky and Suvorov, all great heroes of prerevolutionary Russia. Later, distinctive new uniforms were introduced for officers, complete with epaulettes and gold braid (specially imported from Britain, it is said). On 9 October, at the very height of the battle of Stalingrad, the Soviet government abolished the institution of commissars. This was the system of dual decision-making in the armed forces under which commissars exercised military as well as political control over command decisions. Henceforth officers would take command decisions alone, while the once-powerful political commissars were reduced to the status of advisors on military matters and left to concentrate on propaganda work among the troops.

Such lauding of the officer corps reflected recognition of the importance of this group to the Soviet war effort. During the Great Patriotic War a million officers were killed and another million invalided out of the services. No group was more dedicated or more important to the Soviet victory.

At the supreme command level the professionalisation of Stalin's relations with his generals was another aspect of the increased status and power of the Soviet officer corps. The two key figures were General Alexander M. Vasilevskii, formally appointed Chief of the General Staff on 26 June, and Zhukov, the saviour of Leningrad and Moscow, who was appointed Deputy Supreme Commander of the Soviet armed forces on 26 August 1942. During the course of 1942 Stalin came to rely increasingly on their professional advice, and deferred more and more often to their technical-military judgement. Vasilevskii and Zhukov, together with Stalin, were the architects of the Soviet victory at Stalingrad. An important ingredient of that success was the cohesion, stability and steadfastness of this core group of the supreme command, made possible by Stalin's acceptance of the need for military professionalism.

The contrast with Hitler and the German high command during 1942 could hardly be greater. Hitler increasingly dominated and subordinated his commanders, holding them in even greater contempt than before. Bock's dismissal as commander of Army Group South has already been mentioned. On 24 September – as the battle for Stalingrad raged – Halder was dismissed as Chief of the German Army General Staff and replaced by General Kurt Zeitzler. The ostensible reason for Halder's dismissal was a dispute with Hitler about reinforcements for Army Group Centre, but the root cause was the decision on 23 July to divide the German offensive and to advance on Stalingrad and the Caucasus simultaneously. Halder had not opposed Hitler's will on this matter at the time, but he increasingly feared that its consequence would be German defeat. According to Bernd Wegner, the dismissal is best interpreted as the result of Halder's deliberate provocation of Hitler. By September 1942 the Chief-of-Staff had come to the conclusion that Germany could not now win the war and, unable to influence the course of events, Halder wanted out. As Wegner also notes, Halder's departure was an important landmark in the continuing process of turning the German army into Hitler's personal instrument. Henceforth German strategy became more and more Hitler's personal affair (Boog et al, 2001, pp.1048–59).

The single most important architect of the German defeat at Stalingrad was undoubtedly Hitler. In this respect the decision to split the offensive was a significant turning point. Another watershed was Hitler's persistence in continuing the attack on Stalingrad even when it became clear that the Russians were drawing the German forces into a costly and time-consuming battle of attrition. Albert Seaton spoke for many when he argued:

> 'Hitler's insistence on [Stalingrad's] seizure had little basis in reason, since its capture by the Germans did not assist the destruction of the Red Army west of the Don or further the occupation of the Caucasus ... The holding of the landbridge between the Don and the Volga offered an advantage in that it gave some security to the northern flank, and cutting of the Volga river traffic was of great importance ... There was, however, no reason why the landbridge should not have been seized to the south of Stalingrad or why the Volga should not have been cut further down stream ...' (1971, p.269)

On the other hand, the Germans came very close indeed to winning the battle for the city. In that event Hitler would have been the hero not the villain, not least in the eyes of those many generals who queued up after the war to blame the whole sorry affair on the *Führer*. Most important, battles are won as well as lost. Whatever Hitler's mistakes, whatever the German army's failings, problems and drawbacks, and however close it got to victory, it was the Red Army's successful defence of the city that won the day. The Soviet defensive victory at Stalingrad was very much against the military odds and against expectations when the siege began in earnest at the end of August 1942.

chapter four

STATE OF SIEGE:

SIEGE:

Stalingrad,
September – October
1942

The German assault on Stalingrad began on 23 August 1942 with massive air raids. For two days the *Luftwaffe* pounded the city, flying more than 2000 sorties. According to official Soviet figures the death toll was 40,000. A more conservative estimate would be 25,000. In any event, as Alan Clarke says: 'it was a pure terror raid; its purpose to kill as many civilians as possible, overload all the services, sow panic and demoralisation, to place a blazing pyre in the path of the retreating army' (1965, p.218). General Wolfram von Richthofen, head of the *Luftwaffe's* 8th Air Corps, flew over the battered city and noted in his diary that Stalingrad was 'destroyed and without any further worthwhile targets.' (Hayward, 1998, p.189.) Richthofen was a veteran of the German 'Condor Legion', which had bombed Guernica during the Spanish Civil War, so he was probably a good judge of these matters.

Initially, Stalin forbade evacuation of civilians from the city. 'We shall evacuate nothing', he said. 'We must tell the army and the people that there is nowhere left to retreat. We must defend Stalingrad.' (Harrison, 1985, p.80.) Stalin also considered it important for morale that Soviet forces defend a live city not a deserted one.

Remarkably, Stalingrad continued to function as a city throughout the battle, despite the fact that 90 per cent of it was destroyed during the course of three months of fighting. Electricity continued to be generated, factories continued to turn out tanks and munitions, repair shops and yards continued with their work. However, while many thousands of civilians continued to live among its ruins, most of the city's several hundred thousand civilians were evacuated after the *Luftwaffe* raids. But not everyone escaped. A thousand civilians died when the *Josef Stalin* was sunk while crossing the Volga. Several thousand were caught and executed by the Germans and tens of thousands transported to Germany as slave labourers.

The day the air raids began, units of the German 6th Army reached the Volga at Rynok and Spartakanovka, northern suburbs of Stalingrad. General Fredrich Paulus, commander of the 6th Army, was under orders to take the city quickly by storm. However, difficult terrain and stiff resistance from retreating Soviet armies slowed down the German advance and it wasn't until early September that the main body of 6th Army reached the outskirts of central Stalingrad. Attacking Stalingrad from the south, General Hermann Hoth's 4th Panzer Army ran into similar difficulties and didn't reach the Volga at Kuporosnoye until 10 September. Now Stalingrad was cut off in all directions except east across the Volga, and the defending Soviet armies – the 62nd in the centre and north of the city, the 64th in the southern suburbs – had been separated from each other.

The Soviets feared the city might fall immediately. On 25 August Stalingrad was declared to be in a state of siege and subject to martial law. The next day the city's Communist Party called all citizens to arms: 'We will not surrender our native city, our native home, our native land. We will fill every street in the city with impassable barricades. We will make every house, every block, every street into an impregnable fortress ... Everyone to build barricades! Everyone who can carry a gun to the barricades, in defence of our native city and our native home.' (Samsonov, 1968, pp.152–3.)

At the end of August, Zhukov, the Soviets' newly-appointed deputy Supreme Commander, was sent to Stalingrad to survey the scene himself. On 3 September Stalin sent him an urgent instruction:

> 'The situation is getting worse. The enemy is [two miles] from Stalingrad. They can take Stalingrad today or tomorrow . . . Get the commanders of the troops to the north and north-west of Stalingrad to attack the enemy without delay . . . No delay can be tolerated. Delay at this moment is equivalent to a crime. Throw in all aircraft to help Stalingrad. In Stalingrad itself there is very little aviation left.' (Erickson, 1975, p.384)

As for Hitler, on 2 September he issued an order that when the city was taken the entire male population was to be liquidated and all the females deported. Like Leningrad and Moscow, Hitler wanted Stalingrad to be erased from the face of the earth.

But, before that final solution could be imposed on the city, the Germans had to capture it. The first problem they faced, as Stephen Walsh points out (2000, p.52), was that as they were unable to employ their favourite tactic of the *Kesselschlacht* – the battle of encirclement. Stalingrad was a long, very narrow city that stretched for some 30–40 miles along the western bank of the Volga. Little development had spilled over to the east bank because the Volga was too broad, up to a mile wide at some points. Stalingrad was too extensive to be easily enveloped by German forces who were already over-extended and at the end of very long supply lines, and who would be subject to strong opposition from Soviet divisions protecting the city's flanks along the river's banks. On the other hand, the city's narrowness (never more than 4 or 5 miles wide) invited a direct frontal assault with the aim of breaking through to the riverbank across a broad front.

An alternative tactic, much canvassed after the event, would have been to attack from the north and south along the Volga with the aim of taking control of the riverfront and isolating the defending Soviet forces within the city. But attacking on such narrow fronts would have had its own problems and would have been fiercely contested by the Soviets, who well understood the importance of control of the river bank, the lifeline for their armies in Stalingrad. Besides, the Germans expected to take Stalingrad quickly, if not easily, whatever method they adopted, and they almost succeeded in doing so.

Stalingrad was a city of three main sections (see Map 5, p.xxiii). In the south was the old town, which bordered on the city's railway stations and the central landing stage river dock area. In the central section was a modern city centre with wide boulevards, department stores, civic buildings and public amenities. The north of the city was dominated by three huge factories along the river front: the Dzerzhinskii Tractor factory, which had been converted to tank production; the Barrikady ordnance works; and the Krasnii Oktyabr (Red October) metal plant. Important features of the city from a military point of view were:

(a) the high banks of the Tsaritsa River, which flowed into the Volga and bisected the southern section of the city;

(b) Mamayev Kurgan – an ancient burial mound and, at over 300 feet, one of the highest hills in the city, with commanding views of the centre and north of Stalingrad and across the Volga; and

(c) the defensive shelter offered by the high banks and bluffs of the west side of the Volga, which rose to 1000 feet in places.

The main German attack force was Paulus's 6th Army – the strongest field army in the *Wehrmacht* – conqueror of Poland, France and the Ukraine. Supporting the 6th Army was the 4th Panzer Army, making a total of 21 enemy divisions attacking in the Stalingrad region, although many units were under strength by the time they had fought their way to the Don and Volga. According to Soviet figures, 13 of these enemy divisions (170,000 men, 500 tanks and 3000 artillery pieces) were deployed on the 40-mile front of Stalingrad and its environs. Air support was provided by the *Luftwaffe's* 8th Air Corps, which had about 1000 planes. Facing the Germans was a Soviet force of 90,000, with 2000 artillery pieces, 120 tanks and just under 400 planes.

The same imbalance of forces prevailed on the narrower front of the city of Stalingrad itself. On its 25-mile front the Soviet 62nd Army – the main defending force in the city – was 54,000 strong (as against 100,000 Germans), had 900 artillery pieces (against 2000), and 110 tanks (facing 500). The size and composition of both armies fluctuated, depending on casualties and replacements, but those kind of numbers and force ratios prevailed throughout most of the battle that was to follow.

The two main commanders were Paulus, and, on the Soviet side, General Vasilii Chuikov, who took charge of the 62nd army on 12 September. Paulus is a controversial figure (as losing generals often are) but the consensus is that he was a highly-competent but unimaginative staff officer, an operational technician rather than a field commander, at least not one to be involved in a *Rattenkrieg* (rats' war) as the German soldiers in Stalingrad called the battle. Chuikov, on the other hand, may have lacked operational refinement but he was a tough and determined fighter, independent, outspoken and abrasive – and universally acclaimed as the ideal commander for a brutal and wearying city scrap. The contrast between the two is summed up by the fact that throughout the battle Chuikov was in the thick of it, often under direct fire, his command headquarters pushed back to the water's edge of the Volga, while Paulus (not unreasonably) stayed away from the combat zone and commanded his troops from the rear.

Despite their superior numbers and firepower, the Germans were being drawn into a battle that would involve them in a very different kind of fighting from that with which they were familiar. Much of Stalingrad already lay in ruins following extensive aerial and artillery bombardment. The rubble would obstruct concentrated, mobile attacks by combined air, armour and infantry, while providing cover for defenders. Though out-numbered and out-gunned the defenders would have many advantages in the close combat of the innumerable small battles fought among the city's ruins.

General Hans Doerr, who fought at Stalingrad, was the author of one of the earliest German studies of the battle: *Campaign to Stalingrad* (*Der Feldzug nach Stalingrad*, 1955). In a celebrated passage he set the scene for what was to come:

> 'The battle for the industrial area of Stalingrad, which began in the middle of September, can be described as "trench" or "fortress" warfare. The time for conducting large-scale operations was gone for ever; from the wide expanses of the steppe-land, the war moved into the jagged gullies of the Volga hills with their copses and ravines, into the factory area of Stalingrad, spread out over uneven, pitted, rugged country, covered with iron, concrete and stone buildings. The mile, as a measure of distance, was replaced by the yard ...
>
> For every house, workshop, water-tower, railway embankment, wall, cellar and every pile of ruins, a bitter battle was waged ... The distance between the enemy's army and ours was as small as it could possibly be. Despite the concentrated activity of aircraft and artillery, it was impossible to break out of the area of close fighting ...' (Chuikov, 1963, p.135)

The Stalingrad city battle had four main phases, each dominated by German efforts to break through Soviet defences and occupy the west bank of the Volga (see Map 5, p.xxiii).

During the *first phase,* which began on 13 September, the battle concentrated in the south and centre of the city. German aims were to seize control of the city south of the Tsaritsa river, to occupy the central landing stage of the river dock area, and to split the 62nd Army in two. North of the

Tsaritsa, the aims were to occupy the city centre and to capture the dominating heights of the ancient burial mound of Mamayev Kurgan. By 26 September Paulus was able to declare the south and centre of the city won and announce that 'the battle flag of the Reich flies over the Stalingrad Party building!'. However, although the Germans had reached the Volga and brought the central landing stage area under fire they did not securely occupy it. More important, although the high ground of Mamayev Kurgan had been taken, the Soviets had counter-attacked and it remained contested ground.

The *second phase* of the battle, from 27 September to 7 October, saw the fight for control of Mamayev Kurgan continued, but the main struggle was waged in the north for control of the factory area. The Germans occupied much of the residential district adjacent to the factory area but they failed to take either the factories themselves or their crucial frontage on the Volga – frontage which had become the main conduit from the east bank of the river for reinforcements and supplies to the 62nd Army.

Following a lull in the fighting, the *third phase* of the main battle began on 14 October with a renewed assault on the factory district. By the end of that month the Germans had taken the Dzerzhinskii Tractor factory, the Barrikady and most of Red October. Chuikov's forces were squeezed into a strip on the west side of the Volga that was in places only hundreds of yards across.

Finally, on 11 November Paulus launched his last serious offensive in Stalingrad. Again the target was the factory district and the Germans achieved some success in breaking through to the Volga and occupying another section of the west bank thereby splitting the 62nd Army into three. But the offensive petered out within a couple of days. Chuikov was able successfully to counter-attack in some places and Soviet positions, albeit reduced, remained firm and stable.

By mid-November the Germans occupied more than 90 per cent of Stalingrad. Paulus's men controlled about four miles of riverbank in the northern part of the city and some more river frontage in the south of the city. But, crucially, Chuikov's 62nd Army remained entrenched in a 16-mile strip in the city alongside the Volga's west bank.

On 8 November Hitler spoke to party veterans at the annual reunion in Munich in commemoration of the attempted Nazi putsch there in 1923:

'I wanted to get to the Volga at a certain point near a certain town. As it happens, its name is that of Stalin himself. But please do not think I marched there for that reason – it could be called something quite different – I did so because it is a very important place. Thirty million tons of transport can be cut off there, including nine million tons of oil. All the wheat from the vast Ukraine and the Kuban area converges there to be transported north. Manganese ore is mined there; it is a huge reloading point. I wanted to take it and, you know, we are being modest, for we have got it! There are only a few small places left not captured. Now others are saying: "Why don't you fight more quickly then?" Because I do not want a second Verdun there but I prefer to do it with quite small detachments of assault groups. Time is no object here. Not a single ship is now getting up the Volga and that is the decisive thing!' (Noakes & Pridham, 1988, p.842)

Hitler's reference to Verdun was not his alone. At the time, Stalingrad as the 'Verdun on the Volga' was a common analogy in the world's press. In 1916 the Germans had suffered nearly 300,000 casualties at Verdun in an exhausting and vain effort to take the French city-fortress. But if that is what Hitler wanted to avoid in Stalingrad, it was already too late. By mid-November the German attempt to take Stalingrad was spent. Paulus had lost tens of thousands of men but still did not control the city and was now in no position to take it. What forces he had left were battered and exhausted, and incapable of serious offensive action in the city. Winter had begun and there was no choice except to dig into defensive positions until the spring. The same was true for German forces all along the Eastern Front, including Army Group A in the Caucasus, whose own offensives had petered out by the middle of September.

The battle in Stalingrad had been about who would control the river frontage on the west bank of the Volga. While Chuikov's 62nd Army occupied the riverfront, replacements, ammunition, vodka (lots!), food and medical supplies could be ferried across from the Soviet-controlled east bank. The Germans kept the Volga under artillery fire and air attack but it wasn't enough to stop the river traffic, which in any case moved mainly at night. And while the 62nd Army was entrenched and resupplied on the west bank of the Volga the German position in Stalingrad remained under constant threat of counter-attack. By hanging on in Stalingrad and avoiding complete defeat, Chuikov had effectively won the battle for the city.

There were three 'objective' reasons for Chuikov's success: battle tactics; timely arrival of reinforcements; and artillery and air support. Chuikov is generally acknowledged as the tactical genius who won the battle within Stalingrad. Although recognised as a great commander at the time, his modern-day reputation is based mainly on his memoirs, which were first published in Russian in 1959 and then in English in 1963. Read any account of the battle for Stalingrad and the chances are that much of it will be based on Chuikov's memoirs.

Chuikov's task was to defend Stalingrad at all costs. There was to be no surrender and no retreat. 'For us there is no land across the Volga', became the slogan of his army. According to his own account, Chuikov had no fixed ideas about tactics in the battle. These were worked out on the basis of experience. The first thought that occurred to him, he says, was that a good way to reduce the significance of the Germans' air superiority was by minimising the distance between the forward positions of the opposing forces. 'It occurred to us . . . that we should reduce the no-man's land as much as possible – to the throw of a grenade.' In those circumstances *Luftwaffe* pilots would be reluctant to bomb enemy front-line positions for fear of hitting their own men (the 'friendly fire' problem, as it is called nowadays). A second idea came from the experience of extended fighting around the central railway station in mid-September. In this engagement small groups of soldiers established highly effective strongpoints – mini-fortresses – from which to attack and harry the enemy from all directions. Chuikov arrived at this conclusion:

> 'City fighting is a special kind of fighting. Things are settled here not by strength, but by skill, resourcefulness and swiftness. The buildings in a city are like breakwaters. They broke up the advancing enemy formations and made their forces go along the street. We therefore held on firmly to strong buildings, and established small garrisons in them, capable of all-round fire if they were encircled ... In our counter-attacks we abandoned attacks by entire units and even sections of units. Towards the end of September storm groups appeared in all regiments; these were small but strong groups ... When the Germans occupied an object, it was quickly subjected to attack by storm groups ... Fighting went on for buildings and in buildings – for a cellar, for a room, for every corner is a corridor.' (1963, p.146)

Passages like this are highly reminiscent of articles on the battle in Stalingrad published regularly in the Soviet press in September and October 1942. This suggests that the 62nd Army's tactics were much more a collective innovation than Chuikov's account would lead one to suppose. At the same time, there can be no doubt about the importance of Chuikov's personal persistence and ruthlessness in applying the new tactics. In line with the tactic of using 'storm groups', on 26 September Chuikov issued an order:

> 'I again warn the commanders of all units and formations not to carry out operations by whole units like companies and battalions. The offensive should be organised chiefly on the basis of small groups, with tommy-guns, hand-grenades, bottles of

incendiary mixture [i.e. 'Molotov Cocktails'] and anti-tank rifles.' (*ibid.*, p.150)

Chuikov is at pains to emphasise that the 62nd Army's defence of Stalingrad was an *active* defence based on counter-attacks by his storm groups, a point underlined by General Alexsandr Rodimtsev, the commander of the most famous division to fight at Stalingrad – the 13th Guards:

> 'The fighting ... could be termed defensive only with certain qualifications: it was accompanied by vicious clashes for tactically important buildings and strongpoints. Our constant aim was to impose this combat on the enemy, snatch the initiative from him and force him to assume the defence.' (*Two Hundred Days of Fire*, 1970, p.171)

In his memoirs Chuikov emphasises the difference between Soviet and German tactics and, naturally, the prowess of his men in the battle for the city. But the Germans learnt from experience too and it is clear from detailed accounts of many actions that they adopted much the same house-to-house fighting tactics as the Soviets. Overall German strategy was somewhat different, but that was to be expected of the attacking force. Ironically, when the tables were turned in Berlin in 1945 and Chuikov was attacking that city, he used the same conventional methods as Paulus had at Stalingrad – superior numbers, concentrated firepower, rapid breakthroughs to occupy and hold ground – while small groups of Germans defended from strongpoints in the rubble.

Important though Chuikov's tactical innovations and

leadership were, the 62nd Army would not have survived without the arrival of timely reinforcements at the most critical moments of its battle for survival in Stalingrad.

The first and most important reinforcement came with the arrival of Rodimtsev's 13th Guards Division on 14–15 September. 'Guards' divisions were elite formations, experienced and proven in combat. They were generally bigger and better supplied than ordinary divisions and Guards soldiers enjoyed higher rates of pay. Rodimtsev's troops went straight into action in the city centre and in the fight to retake the high ground of Mamayev Kurgan. On its first day in action the 10,000-strong 13th Guards suffered 30 per cent casualties; during the division's first week in Stalingrad this figure rose to 80 per cent. By the time the battle ended the division had only 320 survivors. As Chuikov wrote in his memoirs: 'had it not been for Rodimtsev's division the city would have fallen completely into enemy hands approximately in the middle of September.' (1963, p.205.)

A second timely intervention was the arrival on 23 September of the 2000-strong 284th Siberian Division led by Lieutenant-Colonel Nikolai Batyuk, which went into action in the area of the central landing stage. Then, on 27–28 September General F.N. Smekhotorov's 193rd Division arrived to take part in the struggle for the factory district. Next General S.S. Guriev's 39th Guards Division and General L.N. Gurtiev's 308th Division crossed the Volga on 1 October to contest the Germans for the Barrikady ordnance works and the Red October metal plant. On 2–3 October the 37th Naval Guards Division commanded by

General Viktor Zholudev was sent in to defend the Tractor factory. Joining in the fray on 16 October was Colonel I.I. Ludnikov's 138th Division and, on 27 October, the 45th Division commanded by Colonel V. P. Sokolov. All these units suffered a similar level of casualties to those of Rodimtsev's 13th Guards i.e. virtual wipe-out. As Chuikov told Alexander Werth shortly after the battle there was no division which by its sacrifices had not saved Stalingrad at one time or another (Werth, 1964, p.509).

It is often said that Stalin and the *Stavka* drip-fed just enough reinforcements to Chuikov to enable the 62nd Army to survive in Stalingrad and wear down the Germans, while holding back most reserves for the counter-offensive they were planning. It is unlikely, however, that such precise calculation was the governing factor in the replenishment of the 62nd Army. The Soviet leadership hoped to hang on in Stalingrad but had no certainty of doing so until the end of October, when the German onslaught in the city began to fade. A series of defeats, from the ill-fated attempt to retake Kharkov onwards, had cost *Stavka* most of its readily available reserves and it took time to form and train new divisions, which were in demand on many fronts, not only in Stalingrad. The possibilities for reinforcing the 62nd Army were limited, particularly in the crucial early days of September and October, when Soviet recovery from the defeats of summer 1942 was just getting underway. There were also logistical problems with transporting forces to and across the Volga when under constant enemy fire. Finally, only so many troops could be deployed in the increasingly narrow ground held by the 62nd Army. Barely enough reinforcements did arrive just in time, but luck was probably more important than fine judgement by the Soviet leadership.

As important as timely reinforcement in saving Stalingrad was artillery and air support. Along the banks of the Volga there were numerous batteries of Soviet artillery. On the east bank opposite Stalingrad there were more than 100 guns per kilometre, including 200 heavy long-distance guns. These rained down shell-fire on German positions in the city pinpointed by Soviet forward observers. Particularly important was accurate shelling of German units in the city as they concentrated for attack on Soviet positions.

Antony Beevor reports that 'the only artillery batteries to remain on the west bank were Katyusha rocket launchers mounted on lorries. Hidden beneath the high Volga bank, they would reverse out to the water's edge, fire their sixteen rockets in rapid succession, then drive back in again.' (1998, p.152.) In the 1960s Konstantin Simonov, a frontline observer of the battle, recalled:

> 'We could certainly not have held Stalingrad had we not been supported by artillery and katyushas on the other bank all the time. I can hardly describe the soldiers' love for them ... And as time went on, there were more and more and more of them, and we could feel it. It was hard to imagine at the time that there was such a concentration of guns firing their shells at the Germans, morning, noon and night, over our heads!' (Werth, 1964, pp.417–18)

In the skies above Stalingrad the Soviet 16th Air Army did battle with the *Luftwaffe*. According to its commander, Air Marshal Sergei I. Rudenko, the Soviet aircraft 'made 77,000 operational flights in defence of Stalingrad, during which they dropped 28,000 tons of bombs, fired 38,000 rockets, about 1.2 million shells and over four million cartridges. In the air and at airfields over 2100 enemy aircraft were destroyed.' (*Two Hundred Days of Fire*, 1970, p.133)

German sources suggest a rather less rosy picture of the defensive air battle than this. According to historian Joel Hayward, the *Luftwaffe's* 8th Air Corps 'contributed significantly to the army's progress within the city, conducting massive attacks on Soviet pockets of resistance' (1998, p.201). But there were significant weaknesses in the German air campaign. The *Luftwaffe* had no night-time bombing capacity. German planes were unable to interdict effectively the flow of supplies across the Volga. The Germans dropped tens of thousands of tons of bombs on Stalingrad but most explosions contributed little more than reconfiguration of existing rubble. Ultimately the pattern in the air was the same as on the ground: the *Luftwaffe* won many victories but failed to win the all-important battle of attrition. The longer the battle continued, the weaker the *Luftwaffe*, and the stronger the Red Air Force became. By the time of the Soviet counteroffensive in November 1942 the Germans had lost their air superiority in the Stalingrad theatre.

While the battle raged in and over the city an important, but generally unsung, battle was also being waged on the flanks of Stalingrad. Soviet units launched many attacks north and south of the city in an effort to pin down German forces and relieve the pressure on the embattled 62nd Army. The Germans did likewise in an effort to ease Paulus's path to success.

According to one estimate (Walsh, 2000, p.99) in the second half of October alone the Germans destroyed the equivalent of seven Soviet divisions in Stalingrad, 75 per cent of Chuikov's strength. Yet still the 62nd Army's will to resist did not crack. As Richard Overy says: 'how the Red Army survived in Stalingrad defies military explanation' (1997, p.175). So what other forces were at work? Beyond tactics, firepower and force ratios, there was the role played by morale, psychology and the human spirit.

In recent years it has become fashionable to downplay the heroism, resilience and determination of the Soviet defence of Stalingrad. Instead, the role of draconian discipline is emphasised. With Soviet security forces in the rear waiting to shoot deserters what choice did the front-line troops have but to fight? The fighting in Stalingrad was mostly a desperate struggle for survival, it is said, not a glorious last redoubt. Like all soldiers the Soviets fought for themselves and their comrades, not for some higher cause. Or maybe it was the vodka that gave the Russians their courage? Certainly the many surreal battle scenes have an aura of drunken haze about them!

It wasn't all heroics and no doubt factors like discipline and desperation played their part. But they alone do not constitute a credible explanation for the 62nd Army's capacity and will to sustain its action in the face of such high casualties.

The vital factor was the politics and psychology of patriotic defence against a murderous enemy that threatened total destruction of *Rodina* – of one's native land. As Elena Senyavskaya puts it in a more general context: 'the outcome of any war is determined in the end by people. The Great Patriotic War of the Soviet people against fascist Germany shows this especially clearly. In the scales of history a whole complex of economic, political and strategic factors on both sides have to be weighed, but the moral-psychological superiority of Soviet soldiers proved to be the weightiest factor of all.' (1999, p.190.)

The role played by Soviet propaganda in the formation and shaping of the attitudes and ethos of what Senyavskaya calls the 'front-line generation' of the Great Patriotic War should not be underestimated, least of all in relation to the battle of Stalingrad.

As the battle developed in September–October 1942 Soviet writers and journalists flocked to the city. Among the better-known observers of the front-line battle in the city were Ilya Ehrenburg, Konstantin Simonov and Vasilii Grossman. But there were many other lesser-known Soviet reporters and journalists there as well. As Alexander Werth points out (1946, p.228 *et seq.*) it was in the *contemporary* reports and writings of Soviet publicists that the Stalingrad 'legend' was born: images of a city landscape of shattered buildings, twisted metal and smoking ruins; the feeling evoked by intense, ferocious, close combat under conditions of constant fire and bombardment; and, above all, stories of unsurpassable individual and collective heroism. Contributing greatly to the legend, too, was fantastic film footage of the street-to-street, house-to-house fighting in Stalingrad screened in Soviet newsreels and documentaries.

Like many legends, this epic tale of heroic Stalingrad has a lot of truth in it. Soviet propaganda reflected, as well as exaggerated, the reality. It also helped to create the reality. The stories, reports and images appearing in the Soviet press were aimed at the front-line troops in Stalingrad as well as at foreign and domestic audiences. The message to participants and observers alike was that this was a struggle of unimaginable horror and difficulty demanding unprecedented courage and commitment – a feat being performed on a daily basis by the embattled Soviet defenders of Stalingrad.

There was more than a little romanticism in the Soviet presentation of the struggle, but what made the message so powerful and vivid was the authenticity of the battle scenario reportage. An early report was by Akulshin and Kuprin in *Pravda* on 21 September:

> 'The Battle of Stalingrad is gaining daily in intensity and fury. Day and night the guns roar at the outskirts of Stalingrad, shells and mines are exploding, and the earth shakes with the sticks of falling bombs. In this constant roar the clatter of tommy-gun and machine-gun fire is lost, and you can hardly hear the sound of rifle-shots. The neighbourhood of the town is wrapped in clouds of smoke, and the flames of burning houses can be seen at night for miles. The outskirts are ploughed up with bomb-craters and shell-holes. In the centre, in the squares and streets, everything speaks of the continuous bombing and of the

shelling by long-range guns ... The roads to Stalingrad are crammed with mountains of scrap metal, remnants of hundreds of smashed vehicles, tanks, guns and mortars.' (Werth, 1946, p.230)

On 28 September the same two reporters wrote in *Pravda*:

'On the banks of the Volga the roar and thunder of the street-fighting resounds like an echo. This ceaseless chaos of earsplitting noises, fire, and smoke, remind one of a gigantic infernal smithy. The fighting for Stalingrad is becoming more bloody and ferocious every day. The whole city shakes with the explosions of shells and mines. The streets are smothered in smoke and clouds of dust that never seem to have time to settle down before another bomb or shell falls.' (ibid, 1946, p.231)

A particular theme of Soviet coverage of the battle were accounts of specific actions by individual units. The exploits of Rodimtsev's 13th Guards received a lot of attention at the time, as they did in post-war Soviet literature on 'heroic Stalingrad'. One of Rodimtsev's heroes was Sergeant Jacob Pavlov. After its officer was killed, Pavlov led a platoon which established a strongpoint in an L-shaped apartment block in central Stalingrad. Despite massive German attacks, Pavlov and his men held out for 58 days in what became known as 'Pavlov's House'. (The remains of the house are preserved as a monument in present-day Volgograd.)

Nowadays a better-known hero is Vasily Zaitsev, the Stalingrad sniper responsible, it is said, for 300 enemy casualties. Zaitsev, who served with Batyuk's 284th Siberian

Division, was the exemplar for a Soviet 'sniperist' movement, which proved very effective in Stalingrad and elsewhere. Zaitsev's more recent fame is the result of the film *Enemy at the Gates* (2001) in which his character is pitted against a German expert sniper who is sent to Stalingrad to take our Soviet hero out. The story of this individual duel was originally popularised by Chuikov in his memoirs. However, as Antony Beevor unsportingly points out (1998, p.204) the story is most likely a myth.

A writer who specialised in portraits of heroic Stalingrad was Vasilii Grossman, the army newspaper *Red Star's* chief correspondent during the siege of the city. One of his most famous pieces was 'The Direction of the Main Blow' (*Napravleniye Glavnogo Udara* – usually translated as 'The Line of the Main Drive)' which was widely published in Russian and English during 1942–3. It is an account of the defence of the factory district by the Siberian regiments of Gurtiev's 308th Division. 'Only here, in Stalingrad, do men know what a kilometre means', wrote Grossman. 'It means one thousand metres, a hundred thousand centimetres.' (*Stalingrad*, 1943, p.69.) Grossman's account of the battle that followed was typical of Soviet accounts of the time:

> 'Astonishing to relate [but] every trench, every pill box, every rifle pit and every ruin turned into a stronghold with its own direction and own system of communication ... [The] battle, unparalleled in its ferocity, lasted for several days. It was fought not for individual buildings and shops, but for every step of a staircase, for a corner in some narrow corridor, for separate machine tools and for the passage-way between them, and for

the gas main. Not a single man in the Division yielded an inch of ground in this battle. And if the Germans did succeed in capturing some particular spot, it indicated that not a single Red Armyman had survived there to defend it ... It was as if the dead had passed on their strength to the survivors ...' (*ibid.*, pp.74–5)

At the same time, Grossman shared with Konstantin Simonov an emphasis on the mundane character of Stalingrad heroism:

'Heroism had become part of the life, the style and manner of this Division and its men. Heroism became an everyday affair, a commonplace. There was heroism in everything – not only in the exploits of the combatants, but also in the work of the cooks peeling potatoes under a blasting, scorching fire of thermite shells. Supreme heroism was displayed in the work of the Red Cross nurses – high school girls from Tobolsk ... who dressed the wounds and brought water to wounded men in the height of battle. Yes, if one were to look with the eyes of an onlooker, heroism would be seen in every commonplace movement of the men of this division. It would be seen in Khamitsky, the Commander of the Signallers' Platoon, as he peacefully sat on a slope near the dugout reading a novel while roaring German dive bombers were pounding the earth. It would be seen in Liaison Officer Batrakov as he carefully wiped his spectacles, placed the report in his dispatch case, and set off on his 20-kilometre tramp through the 'Gully of Death' ... It would be seen in Klava Kopylova ... who sat down to type the battle order and was buried under. She was dug out and moved into another bunker to continue her typing, but was buried under and dug out for a second time; undismayed, she moved into a third dugout, finished typing the order and brought it to the Divisional Commander for signature.' (*ibid.*, p.73)

As Grossman's passage indicates, women made a significant contribution to Soviet combat operations, at Stalingrad, as elsewhere on the Eastern Front. A million women served in the Red Army, about half of them on the frontline. As well as auxiliary roles – often the most dangerous of occupations – Soviet women served in the full range of combat capacities Particularly noteworthy at Stalingrad was female service in anti-aircraft batteries protecting the lifeline across the Volga from air attack. More generally, women were one of the mainstays of the Soviet war effort. The number of women working in industry rose from 38 per cent of the total in 1940 to 53 per cent in 1942. In the countryside it was women who brought in the harvest, with the help of old men and young boys (including a certain Mikhail Gorbachev).

As Chuikov unkindly points out (1963, p.205) Grossman didn't actually witness these particular events since the 308th Division was resting up on the east bank of the Volga when he joined them in November 1942. Nevertheless, Grossman, like many other Soviet reporters, did capture the spirit of the Stalingrad defence, a spirit that grew stronger, more defiant and more confident as the battle progressed. Holding out, remaining undefeated, was quite rightly experienced by Soviet participants as a major achievement.

The German experience of Stalingrad was somewhat different. Naturally, German propagandists had their own account of the battle to offer. But they had a problem – it was difficult to square accounts of German exploits and heroics with the plain fact of failure to take the city. This was a city defended by the *Untermenschen*, who should have been swept aside by the might of the all-powerful, all-conquering *Wehrmacht*. Whatever the Nazi propagandists might say, the sustained Soviet defence of the city suggested that the enemy had a cause they thought worth fighting and dying for, which hardly fitted the image of a degenerate, judeobolshevik regime.

The more prolonged the failure to capture the city, and the more wearing, exhausting and damaging the battle of attrition, the greater was the decline of German morale. This can be charted in extracts from the captured diary of Wilhelm Hoffman of the 6th Army's 94th Infantry Division:

> '*September 5.* Our regiment has been ordered to attack Sadovaya Station – that's nearly in Stalingrad. Are the Russians really thinking of holding out in the city itself? ...
>
> *September 8.* Two days of non-stop fighting. The Russians are defending themselves with insane stubbornness ...
>
> *September 11.* Our battalion is fighting in the suburbs of Stalingrad. We can already see the Volga; firing is going on all the time. Wherever you look is fire and flames ... Russian cannon and machine-guns are firing out of the burning city. Fanatics ...
>
> *September 16.* Our battalion, plus tanks, is attacking the [grain] elevator, from which smoke is pouring – the grain in it is burning, the Russians seem to have set it light themselves. Barbarism ... The elevator is occupied not by men, but by devils that no flames or bullets can destroy ...

September 26. Our regiment is involved in constant heavy fighting. After the elevator was taken the Russians continued to defend themselves just as stubbornly. You don't see them at all, they have established themselves in houses and cellars and are firing on all sides, including from our rear – barbarians, they use gangster methods ... Stalingrad is hell ...

October 4. Our regiment is attacking the Barrikady settlement ...

October 17. Fighting has been going on continuously for four days, with unprecedented ferocity. During this time our regiment has advanced barely half a mile. The Russian firing is causing us heavy losses. Men and officers alike have become bitter and silent ...

October 22. Our regiment has failed to break into the factory. We have lost many men; every time you move you have to jump over bodies ... soldiers are calling Stalingrad the mass grave of the Wehrmacht ...

October 27. Our troops have captured the whole of the Barrikady factory, but we cannot break through to the Volga. The Russians are not men, but some kind of cast-iron creatures; they never get tired and are not afraid of fire ...

October 28. Every soldier sees himself as a condemned man. The only hope is to be wounded and taken back to the rear ...

October 30. We have had no rest ... Everyone is depressed. Stalingrad has turned us into beings without feelings – we are tired, exhausted, bitter.'

The source for the diary is Chuikov who says: 'I have in front of me the diary ... It looks impressive, with stout binding. I have the diary in my personal files.' (1963, p.248 and the following pages for the diary extract.) As a source the diary is almost too good to be true, but other descriptions and reports confirm its documentation of the German agony at Stalingrad. Alan Clark quotes the following memorable passage from the diary of Lieutenant Weiner of the 24th Panzer Division:

'We have fought during fifteen days for a single house, with mortars, grenades, machine-guns and bayonets. Already by the third day fifty-four German corpses are strewn in the cellars, on the landings and the staircases ... There is ceaseless struggle from noon to night. From storey to storey, faces black with sweat, we bombard each other with grenades in the middle of explosions, clouds of dust and smoke, heaps of mortar, floods of blood, fragments of furniture and human beings. Ask any soldier what half an hour of hand-to-hand struggle means in such a fight. And imagine Stalingrad; eighty days and eighty nights of hand-to-hand struggles ... Stalingrad is no longer a town. By day it is an enormous cloud of burning, blinding smoke; it is a vast furnace lit by the reflection of the flames. And when night arrives, one of those scorching, howling, bleeding nights, the dogs plunge into the Volga and swim desperately to gain the other bank. The nights of Stalingrad are a terror for them. Animals flee this hell; the hardest stones cannot bear it for long; only men endure.' (1965, p.238)

Terms like 'horrific' and 'barbaric' are sometimes used to describe the fighting in Stalingrad. But such terms are more appropriately applied to terror bombing of civilian populations, mass execution of Jews, or the ghastly treatment of sick and wounded POWs. The close combat of Stalingrad was by its nature bloody and brutal, and as personal as war ever gets. Above all it was intense, prolonged, unrelenting. It was a struggle between committed, even fanatical individuals, but not a clash of barbarians, notwithstanding the barbaric acts committed by some.

In any event, it was certainly nightmarish, and for the Germans their Stalingrad nightmare was about to go from bad to worse. On 19 November the Russians launched their counter-offensive at Stalingrad – Operation Uranus. Within a few days the 6th Army was encircled in Stalingrad. Fighting in the city continued, but for the next three months the main battle the Germans had to wage was against starvation, disease and hypothermia.

Across the whole of the southern front German forces were in retreat. Army Group B was in disarray, while Army Group A fighting in the Caucasus was barely able to escape encirclement by the Soviets. Any realistic hope of capturing control of Soviet oil supplies was gone and the whole point of Operation Blau undermined. On 25 November a second Soviet offensive – Operation Mars – was launched against Army Group Centre in front of Moscow. In the pipeline were Operations Jupiter and Saturn, ambitious Soviet plans for the grand encirclement of both Army Group Centre and Army Group South. The Soviet aim was not just to beat the Germans at Stalingrad but to roll up the whole Eastern Front and advance rapidly to Berlin.

The Red Gods of War were on the march..

chapter five

RED GODS OF WAR:

Soviet victories, German defeats, November 1942 – February 1943

Everyone expected the Red Army to launch a winter offensive to relieve embattled Stalingrad. But no-one expected the scale and scope of the Soviet counter-attack. On 19–20 November three Soviet army groups attacked with a force of nearly three-quarters of a million troops. The plan was not just to envelop the German 6th Army in Stalingrad but to encircle and destroy the Axis armies defending the Germans' flanks in Don country (see Map 7 p.xxv). From there, Soviet forces would strike for Rostov with the aim of cutting off the 450,000 strong Army Group A in the Caucasus. Army Group A, like Army Group B, would then be destroyed and the Soviets could collapse the whole German campaign in the south.

The Soviets had been planning and preparing their counter-blow for some time. From the very beginning of the Stalingrad campaign Soviet strategists had considered their options for counter-attack. It seems that initial plans focused on counter-strikes to relieve the pressure on the Soviet 62nd and 64th Armies retreating towards Stalingrad. But as the Germans were drawn into battle in Stalingrad the prospects for an encirclement operation became more and more apparent. Finally, the *Stavka* settled on Operation Uranus, a plan for an ambitious strategic counter-offensive utilising the combined forces of the South-West, Don and Stalingrad Fronts – 'the three-front undertaking', as the Soviets called it (Erickson, 1975, p.427).

Our knowledge of the planning and decision-making process leading to Operation Uranus comes mainly from Soviet military memoirs. The best-known account is the one given by

Zhukov (1985, pp.93–7). According to Zhukov, on 12 September 1942 he and the Chief-of-Staff, Vasilevskii, met Stalin to discuss the Stalingrad situation. As a result of this meeting, Stalin ordered Vasilevskii and Zhukov to prepare a plan of action. Zhukov continues:

'After discussing all the possible options, we decided to offer Stalin the following plan of action: first, continue to wear down the enemy by an active defence; second, prepare for a counter-offensive that would hit the enemy in the Stalingrad area hard enough to radically change the strategic situation in the south of the country in our favour.'

On the evening of 13 September the two met Stalin again and after some close questioning by the Soviet leader the plan was agreed in principle. As Zhukov himself indicates, this discussion occurred at a very dramatic moment in the battle for Stalingrad: in mid-September the fate of the city hung in the balance and Rodimtsev's 13th Guards were about to be sent across the Volga to save it. In Moscow, however, the leadership kept its head and coolly considered all the options. It's a good story, and one that is repeated throughout the Stalingrad literature. But is it true?

According to Stalin's appointments diary there were no meetings with Vasilevskii and Zhukov on 12 and 13 September 1942. In fact, there is no record of any meeting between Stalin and Zhukov between 31 August and 26 September. Stalin saw Vasilevskii during this period but not on any date between 9 and 21 September. Moreover, we know that for much of September Vasilevskii and Zhukov were not even in Moscow, but visiting the frontline at Stalingrad and elsewhere. In their absence Stalin met regularly with other *Stavka* Staff officers, including, on 13 September, with General Fedor Bokov, the General Staff's political commissar, and it is likely that the Soviet leader was briefed on the evolving plans for the great counter-offensive at Stalingrad; but not, it seems, by Zhukov and Vasilevskii. (The relevant section of the diary was published in *Istoricheskii Arkhiv* (Historical Archives), No.2, 1996, pp.35–8.)

Stalin's 'diary' is a fascinating day-by-day, hour-by-hour record of who he saw, and for how long, not just during the war but throughout his tenure as General Secretary of the Communist Party. Since it only records Stalin's meetings in his Kremlin office, it is not a complete and infallible guide to all his appointments, but by the 1940s Stalin rarely had meetings elsewhere. Zhukov, moreover, is quite specific that the meetings in question took place in Stalin's office.

In his memoirs Vasilevskii subsequently broadly backed up Zhukov's story. But, always more the team player, Vasilevskii counterbalanced his and Zhukov's role with an emphasis on the collective effort that devised the counter-stroke at Stalingrad:

'The strategic plan to defeat the enemy near Stalingrad emerged and matured during fierce defensive fighting on the Volga and was the result of team work involving Supreme Command representatives, General Staff, the echelons of all arms and services and the rear of the People's Commissariat of Defence, Fronts and Army Commands and Staffs.' (*Two Hundred Days of Fire*, 1970, pp.33–4)

Marshal Nikolai N. Voronov, Chief of Soviet Artillery during the war, makes a similar, but more pointedly anti-Zhukov, comment: 'this operation was not the brainchild of one man but the result of extensively creative and minutely concerted activity of a considerable team of generals and officers' (*ibid.*, p.62).

Actually, Vasilevskii was being far too modest. If anyone could take credit as the architect of the Soviet victory at Stalingrad, it was him. As Chief-of-Staff he was involved throughout the planning process and when it came to implementation was posted to the southern front to coordinate and direct operations. But much more important than the wrangle about the precise authorship of Operation Uranus is the story of what David Glantz (1999) calls *Zhukov's Greatest Defeat*.

Uranus had a companion piece – Operation Mars. In fact, Mars was timetabled to start before Uranus, in mid-October, but weather and other factors delayed the operation until the end of November. This was a planned attack against Army Group Centre in front of Moscow, with the initial aim of encircling the German 9th Army in the Rzhev salient (see Map 6, p.xxiv).

The forces allocated to the Mars offensive were equivalent to those earmarked by the *Stavka* for Uranus and, according to

More prosaically, Glantz and House summarise the situation as follows: 'Soviet strategic aims had expanded far beyond the simple defeat of German forces in southern Russia: the Stavka sought to collapse enemy defences along virtually the entire Eastern Front' (1995, p.143). In effect, what the Soviets proposed to do was to win the war in 1943. A Soviet victory over Germany two years before the war actually ended and a year before the D-Day landings in France would, needless to say, have had far-reaching consequences for the future of Europe and for Stalin's role in dictating the terms of the peace.

In Soviet accounts, however, Mars is downplayed and obscured as a diversionary operation to distract German attention and forces away from the Stalingrad theatre. Uranus, it is said time and again, was where the main action took place and was always intended to be. However, as Ziemke and Bauer point out, Uranus was 'a highly speculative venture' (1987, p.445). It depended for its success on two uncertain factors. First, that the 62nd Army could hold out in Stalingrad until Uranus was ready for launch, which at the time the operation was being planned and prepared was doubtful, to say the least. And, second, that the Germans would be unable to evade or break out of the planned encirclements. In the event, the Germans weren't able to escape, but no Soviet planner could have been sure of that in advance. Mars, on the other hand, seemed a more certain proposition. It was an operation in 'the area that, during 1941 and 1942, had consistently been regarded in Soviet thinking as the most important strategic direction, the one in which Soviet forces had already conducted a successful winter offensive and in which they could expect to be able to stage another on better terms than the first.' (*ibid.*)

Ziemke and Bauer also point out that Soviet force disposi-tions along the Eastern Front reinforce this very point. Against Army Group Centre, *Stavka* deployed 1.9 million troops, just under 25,000 artillery pieces, nearly 3500 tanks and more than 1000 aircraft. Against Army Group B – the main target of Uranus – only 1.1 million Soviet troops, 15,500 artillery pieces, 1500 tanks and fewer than 1000 air-craft were deployed. While the force ratios were less favourable to the Soviets in the centre than the south (1.9:1, as opposed to 2:1) and the quality of the opposition better (Army Group Centre relied on few, if any, Axis troops), that could be construed as an argument for defeating the enemy where it really mattered, that is in front of Moscow.

The only problem with Mars was that it failed, and at the cost of nearly 350,000 Soviet casualties, including 100,000 dead. It failed because the Germans expected the major Soviet counter-blow to be in the centre, and they were right! What the Germans miscalculated was the Soviet capacity to launch simultaneously an equally strong operation in the south.

In any event, alert to the danger, with reserves available, and with stronger and better-prepared forces, Army Group Centre was able to defend its positions quite well. By the end of December Mars had been called off well short of achieving its operational goals. The yet more ambitious Operation Jupiter fell by default. By contrast, Uranus succeeded bril-liantly, at least in terms of its initial aim of encircling

Stalingrad. But Saturn, the follow-up operation centred on a drive to Rostov, had to be downgraded to a more defensive operation ('Little Saturn') to deal with German attempts to relieve their forces trapped in Stalingrad. The German relief operation was stopped and the 6th Army remained encircled by the Soviets, but defensive manoeuvres and counter-attacks enabled Army Group A to escape from the Caucasus.

The November counter-offensive at Stalingrad was *the* turning point of the war on the Eastern Front. With victory at Stalingrad the road to Berlin was at last opened up. But Stalingrad was nowhere near as dramatic and decisive a victory as hoped for by the Soviets. It was a radical turning point (*perelom*, as the Russians say) but not an immediately war-winning one. The most ambitious Soviet goals – the goals of Mars, Jupiter and Saturn – remained unrealised.

In retrospect, however, Soviet failures were eclipsed by the stunning success of Uranus in encircling the German and Axis armies at Stalingrad. Soviet leaders subsequently claimed, as generals and politicians usually do of their successes, that what had actually happened was what they had intended all along. Hence the familiar story about Stalingrad as a deliberate trap to lure the Germans in, wear them down and then defeat them. But another story of Stalingrad is the failure of the Soviets to win the great battle that they really wanted to win: the expulsion of all the German armies from central and southern Russia.

Failed or not, over-ambitious or not, the fact that the Red Army could even contemplate such a dual strategic offensive on the central and southern fronts was a telling commentary on the depth and scale of the Soviet recovery from the defeats of summer 1942. This recovery was all the more remarkable given the general situation and condition of the Soviet state by mid-1942.

By the time of Stalingrad the Germans occupied half of European Russia – more than a million square miles of territory. The area contained 80 million people, some 40 per cent of the Soviet population – and nearly 50 per cent of the cultivated land. In industrial terms the occupied area had accounted for the production of approximately 70 per cent of pig iron, 60 per cent of steel and coal, and 40 per cent of electricity. By November 1942 Soviet military casualties since June 1941 (dead, wounded and missing) totalled eight million. The bodies of millions more Soviet citizens lay dead in the German-occupied territories.

Losses of weaponry were equally astronomical: tens of thousands of tanks and planes and scores of thousands of artillery pieces. But by the end of 1942 Soviet annual output of rifles had quadrupled (to nearly six million) compared to 1941, while tank and artillery production had increased fivefold to 24,500 and 287,000 per annum respectively, and the number of planes produced rose from 8200 to 21,700. This achievement was testimony to the mobilising power of the Soviet economy, but also a tribute to the amazing mass dismantlement and relocation of industrial plant to the east that occurred in summer 1941 and again, on a smaller scale, in summer 1942. For example, despite the rapidity of the German advance in the south, the Soviets were still able to evacuate 150 large-scale enterprises from the Don and Volga regions. As well as successfully relocating industry the Soviets created 3500 new factories during the war, most of them dedicated to armaments production.

There is an ongoing debate about the explanation for the success of the wartime Soviet economy. The old official Soviet view was that the USSR's wartime economic mobilisation was made possible by the economy's centralised ownership and control, and by effective planning of resources and outputs. The alternative view is that there was a significant reform of the Soviet economy during the war in the direction of decentralised decision making and the introduction of elements of a market economy, particularly in agriculture and in the urban retail sector. Another angle on the discussion is highlighted by Geoffrey Hosking's comment that 'the planned economy was better at improvising than at planning' (1990, p.282). What he meant by this was that behind the official plans and targets there was much adaptation at the individual and enterprise level. Before the war such improvisation was often aimed at subverting the demands of central authorities and officialdom. During the war such creativity was at the service of the state and of the national war effort. At the same time there was a good deal of continuity between the pre-war and war-time Soviet economies, and more generally. As Robert Service notes: 'already having been a highly "militarised" society before 1941, the USSR became co-ordinated as if it were simply a great armed camp wherein the Red Army itself was but the most forward and exposed contingent.' (1997, p.278.)

Another area of controversy concerns the contribution of western aid to the Soviet war effort. During the war the Soviet regime was fairly fulsome in its praise of western aid support. In the post-war period, however, Moscow was intent on claiming all the credit for the Soviet victory. As always the figures vary, but between 1941 and 1945 the USSR's western allies supplied about 10 per cent of Soviet wartime economic needs. For example, the United States under its lend-lease programme supplied 360,000 trucks, 43,000 jeeps, 2000 locomotives, 11,000 railroad cars, and food that fed about a third of the civilian population. Most of this aid arrived *after* Stalingrad, so it cannot be said to have been crucial to Soviet victory in the war, although it did greatly facilitate the Red Army's march to Berlin. On the other hand, as Mark Harrison (2002) has pointed out, in 1942 the Soviet economy was on a knife-edge of collapse. All support made a crucial difference, including the limited amount of western aid delivered by this time. Western moral support for the Soviet struggle against Germany was also important.

The Germans radically under-estimated the USSR's productive capacity, while their own output of weaponry in 1942 barely matched the 1941 Soviet figures. The same point applied to personnel resources. The Germans had difficulty in maintaining the size of their military establishment (seven to eight million troops) whereas the Soviets, despite massive casualties, increased their numbers by more than 50 per cent in 1942 (from seven to 11 million) On the eve of the Soviet counter-offensive the Germans had virtually no reserves left to defend their position in the southern theatre. The Soviets, on the other hand, were able to deploy an attack force of more than 90 divisions along the frontline of the Stalingrad counter-offensive. Most of this force was fully-equipped and fresh, although the *Stavka* had rotated divisions in and out of the combat zone in order to give them some fighting experience.

Learning from the success of the German surprise attack of 22 June 1942, the deployment of the Soviet attack forces was conducted in conditions of utmost secrecy. Knowledge of the forthcoming operation was kept on a strict need-to-know basis. Troops and supplies were transported to the front at night. The main assault forces were not deployed until the last possible moment. There were active, as well as passive, camouflage measures (what the Soviets called *maskirovka*) i.e. false information and signals designed to convince the Germans that they knew what was going to happen. The main Soviet tactic was to spread the false idea that they were preparing their defences rather than planning a major offensive. As David Glantz says, the Soviets' 'greatest feat was in masking the scale of the [coming] offensive' (1989, p.113). They were aided in this achievement by the German conviction that the main counter-blow would come in the centre, rather than the south and also by the German illusion that Soviet reserves and resources were as depleted as their own. On the eve of the Soviet offensive, General Kurt Zeitzler, the Chief of the German General Staff, stated that 'the Russians no longer have any reserves worth mentioning and are not capable of launching a large scale offensive. In forming any appreciation of enemy intentions, this basic fact must be fully taken into consideration.' (*ibid.* p.117.)

The offensive of which the Soviets were supposedly incapable began on 19 November with an artillery barrage fired by 3,500 guns and mortars. The main attack north of Stalingrad was conducted by the 21st Army and the 5th Tank Army of General Nikolai F. Vatutin's South-Western Front. South of the city the Soviets attacked (on 20 November) with the 51st and 57th Armies of General Andrei I. Yeremenko's Stalingrad Front. This dual attack was supported by the forces of General Konstantin K. Rokossovsky's Don Front. The plan was for Vatutin's forces to advance south-east towards Kalach and for Yeremenko's forces to strike north-west towards the same objective. At the same time an outer defensive line would be established along the Chir and Krivaya rivers. An ambitious double encirclement of (a) the 6th Army and 4th Panzer in Stalingrad and (b) enemy forces in the Don bend was envisaged (see Map 7, p.xxv).

Barring the Soviet advance north of Stalingrad was the Rumanian 3rd Army, a ten-division force of some 100,000 men. South of Stalingrad was the 4th Rumanian Army with seven divisions and 70,000 men. The Soviet forces outnumbered and outgunned the Rumanians by three or four to one. In addition to being out-numbered, the Rumanians were badly supplied, having been starved of resources by the Germans, who had concentrated on supplying their own forces. The Rumanians also had the task of holding long defensive lines on the open steppe with little fortification. Most importantly, the Germans had no real reserves with which to back up the Rumanians.

The Soviet attack made such rapid progress that on 21 November, just two days after the launch of Operation Uranus, Paulus signalled Weichs, the commander of Army

Group B that the 6th Army was 'completely encircled' (Tarrant 1992 p.115). But it wasn't until 23 November that the armies of the South-Western and Stalingrad Fronts linked up at Kalach to complete the envelopment of the 6th Army. The Rumanian divisions in the area of encirclement were virtually destroyed.

A few days later Henry Shapiro, United Press's Moscow correspondent, visited the battlefield. He later told Alexander Werth of:

> 'thousands of Rumanians just wandering about the steppe, cursing the Germans, and looking desperately for Russian feeding-points ... All they wanted was to be formally taken over as war prisoners ... The steppe was a fantastic business. The whole goddam steppe was full of dead horses – some were only half-dead, and it was pathetic to see one standing on three frozen legs, and shaking the remaining one. Ten thousand horses had been killed by the Russians in the breakthrough. The whole steppe was strewn with these dead horses, with gun carriages, wrecked tanks, and guns ... and no end of corpses – Rumanians and Germans ... Kalach was a shambles. Of the whole town only one house was standing, and even it had only three walls. At the headquarters of the local staff, I met the commander, a Colonel, who was a professor of philosophy at the University of Kiev, and we sat up most of the night discussing Kant and Hegel.' (Werth, 1946, pp.355–6)

The perimeter of the encircled area of Stalingrad was about 80 miles long and contained an area ranging from 25–35 miles in breadth and depth (see Map 10, p.xxviii). Surrounding the area were seven Soviet armies with 94 divisions between them. Inside the *Kessel* (the cauldron), as the Germans called it, were 20 divisions of 6th Army and 4th Panzer, two Rumanian divisions and a Croatian infantry regiment. Total manpower was nearly 300,000, with 100 tanks, 1800 artillery pieces, 10,000 vehicles and 23,000 horses. This was nearly three times the enemy force the Soviets expected to bag. Among those trapped were a large number of *Hilfswillige* ('Hiwis' for short – literally, 'willing helpers'). These were mainly Soviet/Russian auxiliaries, mostly former POWs, who had been drafted in to work for the Germans as labourers. Estimates of their numbers range from 20,000 to 50,000. In any event, very few of them lived to tell the tale of their experience in Stalingrad. Those who survived the Germans and the battle were finished off by Soviet security forces.

On the German side the question arose as to whether their forces in Stalingrad should stand fast and fight or attempt a breakout. After the war it became conventional wisdom to blame Hitler for the decision to hold out in Stalingrad, thereby sealing the fate of the 6th Army. However, at the time the picture was more complicated. Certainly Hitler was reluctant to retreat from Stalingrad. He had invested a lot of psychological and political capital in the capture of the city. In October 1942 he had proclaimed: 'where the German soldier sets foot, there he remains ... You may rest assured that nobody will ever drive us away from Stalingrad' (Tarrant, 1992, p.231). Hitler feared that open admission of defeat at Stalingrad would lead to a more general collapse of the German position in the war.

It is also true that many of Hitler's senior commanders,

including Paulus, urged him to allow a breakout operation by the 6th Army. He refused this advice because he was assured by Air Marshal Herman Goering and General Hans Jeschonnek, Chief of the *Luftwaffe* General Staff, that it was possible to airlift sufficient supplies to the 6th Army (although, to be fair, Jeschonnek subsequently changed his mind, and told Hitler so). Equally important was Field Marshal Manstein's advice on 24 November. Following the launch of the Soviet counter-offensive, Manstein, the conqueror of the Crimea, was recalled from the siege of Leningrad to take charge of a newly-created command, Army Group Don, consisting of the 6th Army, 4th Panzer and the 3rd Rumanian Army plus some promised reinforcing divisions. On his return south, Manstein took the position that a rescue operation – not a breakout – was the best option, provided the 6th Army could be adequately supplied by air. The idea was that the Germans would break though the encirclement of Stalingrad from the outside. A corridor to the 6th Army would be created, opening the way for supplies and reinforcements to flow, as well as providing an escape route. Viewed optimistically, as Hitler always viewed his defeats and disasters, the encirclement of the 6th Army was only temporary. If the 6th Army held out and if the breakthrough operation succeeded, there was every prospect that a new, stable defensive line in the south could be established. Hitler even thought that, in due course, it would be possible to remount the Caucasus campaign. His fantasies knew no bounds, it seems.

Adding more realistic weight to the decision to mount a rescue operation were doubts that the 6th Army was in any fit state to break out of its encirclement. It was weak from the gruelling battle for Stalingrad, preparations for a breakout would take time; and any escape attempt would be opposed strongly by the Soviets. Wounded would have to be left behind and equipment abandoned. It would have been a disastrous retreat even had it succeeded.

When the Soviets attacked on 19 November, Hitler was staying at his mountain retreat in Berchtesgaden in southern Bavaria and he did not return to military headquarters at Rastenburg in East Prussia until 23 November. Crucially, while his commanders on the Eastern Front were urging withdrawal of the 6th Army from Stalingrad those with him on holiday went along with his own inclination which, as always, was to stand fast and fight. By the time he got to East Prussia his mind was made up and that coloured his reception of all contra-indications and opinions. Although there were plenty of the latter, none were put with or carried much force. Notwithstanding their later, self-serving claims, the German generals had by this time been reduced to the role of 'highly paid NCOs', as Richthofen, the *Luftwaffe* commander, recorded in his diary on 25 November 1942. Actually, Richthofen was quite outspoken, and more willing than most to stand up to Hitler, and not just in the privacy of his diary. More typical was the sense of diminished responsibility expressed by Manstein in his reply to Paulus on 26–27 November urging him to implement Hitler's directive of 24 November to fight on in Stalingrad:

'The Führer's order relieves you of all responsibility other than the most appropriate and resolute execution of the Führer's order. What happens when, in execution of the Führer's order,

the army has fired off its last bullet – for that you are not responsible!' (Boog et al, 2001, p.1139)

Many of Paulus's senior officers in Stalingrad favoured a
breakout; indeed some began active preparations for such an
operation. Leading this defiance of the Fuhrer's will was
General Walter von Seydlitz-Kurzbach, the commander of 6th
Army's 51st corps. On 25 November he sent a memo to Paulus:

'The [6th] Army is faced with a clear alternative: breakthrough
to the south-west in the general direction of Kotelnikovo or
face annihilation within a few days ... Unless the Army
Command immediately rescinds its order to hold out in a
hedgehog position it becomes our inescapable duty to the army
and to the German people to seize that freedom of action that
we are being denied by the present order, and to take the opportunity which still exists at this moment to avert catastrophe by
making the attack ourselves. The complete annihilation of
250,000 fighting men and their entire equipment is at stake.
There is no other choice.' (Tarrant, 1992, pp.142–3)

The dismissive comment of Paulus's Chief-of-Staff, General
Arthur Schmidt, on this memo was: 'we don't have to break
the head of the Fuhrer for him, and neither does General von
Seydlitz have to break the head of [General Paulus]' ('Wir
haben uns nicht den Kopf des Fuhrers zu zerbrechen und Gen.v.
Seydlitz nicht den des O.B.') (Kehrig, 1974, p.567). More relevant was Paulus's argument in his memoirs that independant
action by the 6th Army would have led to a command crisis
with potentially disastrous consequences. Disobeying orders
was not a realistic option (Göerlitz, 1963, pp.283–5).

Seen in this context Hitler's decision on 24 November to order the 6th Army to remain in Stalingrad was arguably not self-evidently wrong, and far from irrational. However, Hitler's subsequent inflexibility certainly proved disastrous. For a start, the military's view was that Manstein's rescue operation was a way of getting the 6th Army out of the city. For Hitler it became a means to hang on in Stalingrad, a way of executing only a partial withdrawal while at the same time holding on to positions on the Volga. By 12 December Hitler was adamant:

> 'I have, on the whole, considered one thing', he told Zeitzler. 'We must not give [Stalingrad] up now under any circum-stances. We won't win it back again. We know what that means ... to imagine that one can do it a second time, if one goes back and the material is left lying, that's ridiculous. They can't take everything with them ... What isn't brought out by motor will be left behind ... We can't possibly replace the stuff we have inside. If we give that up, we surrender the whole meaning of this campaign. To imagine that I shall come here another time is madness. Now, in winter, we can construct a blocking position with those forces ... We are not coming back here a second time. That is why we must not leave here. Besides, too much blood has been shed for that.' (Boog et al, 2001, p.1148)

Then there was the issue of the airlift. An absolute daily min-imum of 300 tons of supplies was required by the 6th Army and an average of 150 fully laden Ju 52 transport aircraft would need to land in the *Kessel* every day. That meant 800 Ju 52s were required. However, the *Luftwaffe* only had 750 such aircraft in total, and half those were supplying the retreating German armies in North Africa.

As well as being under-equipped the *Luftwaffe* faced recurrent bouts of bad weather (on some days no supplies were landed) and increasingly strong opposition from the Soviet Air Force. In the final reckoning the *Luftwaffe* delivered an average of only 117.6 tons per day during the siege of the 6th Army. Nearly 500 aircraft (Ju 52s and other planes utilised for the airlift) and 1000 airmen were lost (although the Soviets claim much higher figures for enemy losses). The *Luftwaffe* never really recovered from these losses. For its part, the 6th Army starved and grew weaker and more vulnerable every day, its troops less and less able either to defend themselves or to contribute to breaking the Soviet encirclement.

Hitler's final hope was that Manstein's planned breakthrough operation would succeed. Codenamed Operation *Wintergewitter* ('Winter Storm'), this began on 12 December. It consisted of an advance by two divisions of the 57th Panzer Corps from Kotelnikovo towards the *Kessel* about 60 miles away. The operation made some initial progress but soon ran into strong Soviet opposition and within a week or so had ground to a halt on the line of the River Chir, about 25–30 miles from Stalingrad (see Map 8, p.xxvi). At this time (19–23 December) the question of a possible breakout by 6th Army re-emerged. But 6th Army was in no condition to launch such an action unless the relief operation got a lot closer to Stalingrad. By Christmas all hope of either a breakthrough or a breakout had gone. The 6th Army was doomed.

Meanwhile another military crisis for the Germans was gathering pace. Because of the pressure created by Manstein's relief attempt the Soviets had revised their plans for a major drive to Rostov (Operation Saturn). Now their priority was to direct forces to the south-west to attack German Army Group Don and maintain the encirclement of Stalingrad. In an operation called 'Little Saturn' the Soviets hoped to achieve that goal while at the same time preparing the way for a full advance to Rostov. Little Saturn began on 16 December with an attack by three Soviet armies (6th, 1st and 3rd Guards) on the northern flank of Army Group Don. The 11 divisions of the Italian 8th Army guarding the flank were soon reeling and within a few days Mussolini's 200,000+ force was in full retreat (see Map 9, p.xxvii).

The Germans were faced with the imminent danger of the isolation and collapse of Army Group Don. The only way to defend the position was to withdraw the German armies from the Caucasus. According to his own account (1956, p.155), on 27 December, Zeitzler told Hitler that 'unless you order a withdrawal from the Caucasus now, we shall soon have a second Stalingrad on our hands'. Hitler replied: 'very well, go ahead and issue the orders.' The Fuhrer then changed his mind, but it was too late: Zeitzler had already issued the orders. As we shall see in Chapter 6, Manstein was able to salvage the situation and successfully withdraw what remained of the German forces from the southern theatre. That did not include the 6th Army, but even in its death throes it continued to play an important role by tying up significant Soviet forces for another month or so.

By January 1943 the 6th Army's end was in sight. From the German perspective, it was the end of an ordeal and the climax of a tragedy. From the Soviet point of view it was the deserved fate of the would-be conquering army of an exterminationist regime. In the southern campaign as a whole the Soviets suffered 2.5 million casualties in 1942–3. In defending Stalingrad itself there were nearly 650,000 casualties, half of them dead or missing. Within the city limits there lay dead tens of thousands of Soviet soldiers and a similar number of civilians. The Germans could hardly expect much sympathy for their fate from that quarter.

Inside the *Kessel* the entombed 6th Army rotted away. Between 22 November and 7 January more than 50,000 of its members died. Some fell to enemy action, but many succumbed to starvation, disease and frostbite. As Colonel H.R. Dingler of the 3rd Motorised Division recalled:

'The weather conditions were bearable during the first days of December. Later on heavy snowfalls occurred and it turned bitterly cold. Life became a misery ... We were short of all sorts of supplies. We were short of bread and, worse, of artillery ammunition, and worst of all, of gasoline. Gasoline meant everything to us. As long as we had gasoline we were able to keep warm ... Until Christmas, 1942, the daily bread ration issued to every man was 100 grammes. After Christmas the ration was reduced to 50 grammes per head. Later on only those in the forward line received 50 grammes per day. No bread was issued to men in regimental headquarters and upwards. The others were given watery soup which we tried to improve by making use of bones obtained from the corpses of the horses we dug up. As a Christmas treat the army allowed the slaughtering of four thousand of the available horses. My division, being a motorised formation, had no horses and was therefore particularly hard hit, as the horseflesh we received was strictly rationed.' (Tarrant, 1992, pp.178–9)

On 1 January 1943 Hitler messaged Paulus: 'you and your soldiers should begin the New Year with strong faith that I and the High Command ... will use all strength to relieve the defenders of Stalingrad and make their long wait the greatest triumph of German military history'. To his soldiers Hitler said: 'the men of the Sixth Army have my word that everything is being done to extricate them' (*ibid.*, p.182).

In the early days of the encirclement hope of rescue or of a breakout was widespread among the troops. But by the New Year few, if any, of the trapped Germans believed their fate would be other than death or captivity. The only real hope of survival was to be wounded and lucky enough to be flown out, or to have specialist skills deemed too valuable to lose. Some 25,000 of the 6th Army 'escaped' from Stalingrad in this way.

As the end approached more and more Germans in Stalingrad deserted. The great majority of the 6th Army, however, stuck it out to the very end. It was in its own way a noble and heroic sacrifice, a match for the Soviet feats of endurance in the sieges of Leningrad, Sevastopol and Stalingrad. Whether the sacrifice was justified morally or worth it strategically is another question.

Aside from military calculations, Hitler was counting on a great mythical sacrifice that would inspire the remaining

German armies and restore flagging morale on the Eastern Front. Again, Hitler's sense of the psychology of the moment was more acute than posterity has generally credited him. As Gerd Ueberschar argues: 'Stalingrad provided a foretaste of the brutal, senseless fighting that would be continued right to the bitter end of total defeat in May 1945' (Muller and Ueberschar, 1997, p.118). It is often asked why the *Wehrmacht* did not collapse as it retreated to Berlin in 1943–5 and why, with no prospect of anything except death and defeat, the great mass of German soldiers fought to the very end. Part of the answer lies in the inspiration provided by the sacrifice of their comrades in the 6th Army at Stalingrad.

For German propaganda the 6th Army's stand at Stalingrad became the model for the total sacrifice of total war demanded by Goebbels in February 1943. Addressing the Nazi faithful at a mass rally in Berlin, Goebbels told them that 'in this war there will be neither victors nor vanquished, but only survivors and annihilated'. Whipping the crowd up to a fanatical frenzy, he concluded by asking them:

'Is your trust in the Fuhrer greater, more faithful, and more unshakeable than ever? Is your readiness to follow him in all his ways and do everything necessary to bring the war to a triumphant end absolute and unrestricted? Now people, arise – and storm burst forth!'

It was going to be a long, brutal and unremitting struggle all the way to Berlin.

When the Soviets realised the full extent of the force they

had surrounded in Stalingrad, they prepared a major operation to reduce the *Kol'tso* (the Ring), as they called it. But before launching Operation Ring, they offered surrender terms to the 6th Army. In a message to Paulus on 8 January 1943 the Germans were offered food, medical support and POW status if they surrendered. But Paulus was under strict instructions from Hitler to fight to the last man and he was intent on following his orders. The offer was rejected and on 10 January the Soviets began their attack.

The seven Soviet armies surrounding the *Kol'tso* were commanded by Rokossovsky and by Voronov, who represented the *Stavka*. Under their command was a force of 280,000 with 250 tanks and 10,000 artillery pieces and mortars, supported by 400 planes from the 16th Air Army. Among the formations taking part in the attack was the much-recovered and replenished 62nd Army commanded by Chuikov. The Soviet force was more than a match for the resource-starved and emaciated Germans, who by this time had only 25,000 functioning front-line troops.

The Red Armies drove deep into the *Kessel*, aiming to split the defence of the encircled area (see Map 10, p.xxviii). By 16 January Pitomnik, the Germans' main airfield inside the *Kessel*, had fallen to the Soviets. The other German airfield, Gumrack, fell on 23 January. Fittingly, the Germans were forced to retreat to the ruins of the city, and by 26 January Paulus's forces had been split in two, and then in three, much like Chuikov and the 62nd Army only a short time previously. Ziemke and Bauer describe the scene in Stalingrad itself:

'As the front fell back from the west, the inner city, which after months of bombardment had the appearance of a landscape in hell, became a scene of fantastic horror. Sixth Army reported twenty thousand uncared-for wounded and an equal number of starving, freezing and unarmed stragglers. Those who could took shelter in the basements of the ruins, where tons of rubble overhead provided protection against a constant rain of artillery shells. There, in the darkness and cold, the sick, the mad, the dead and the dying crowded together, those who could move daring not to for fear of losing their places.' (1987 p.499)

On 17 January the Soviets renewed their offer of surrender terms to the Germans, and did so again on 25 January. On 22 January Paulus sent a message to Hitler reporting on the desperate situation of his army and hinted at the possibility of surrender. But Hitler refused to countenance capitulation: 'surrender is out of the question. The troops will defend themselves to the last' (*ibid.*, p.499). Paulus in turn told his men: 'Hold on! If we cling together as a sworn community and if everyone has the fanatical will to resist to the utmost, not to be taken prisoner under any circumstances, but to persevere and be victorious, we shall succeed.' (Boog et al, 2001, p.1163.) On 29 January Paulus sent this message to Hitler on the eve of the tenth anniversary of the Nazi takeover in Germany: 'may our struggle be an example to the present and future generations never to capitulate, even in the most hopeless situation. By such means Germany will be victorious' (*ibid.*, p.1164). On this occasion Goering gave the anniversary speech. He said of Stalingrad: 'a thousand years hence Germans will speak of this battle with reverence and awe, and will remember that in spite of everything

Germany's ultimate victory was decided there' (Tarrant, 1992 p.218).

Seydlitz and other commanders advised Paulus to stop the fighting but he would not do so. In fact the high command of the 6th Army never did formally surrender their forces. It was left to junior officers to negotiate a *de facto* capitulation. Even after capture by the Soviets, Paulus refused to sign or issue orders to his men to lay down their arms. To his befuddled Soviet captors he explained that he was unable to issue such orders now that he was a POW!

As Bernd Wegner has commented, there was more to Paulus's obstinate refusal to surrender than a warped sense of military honour and discipline. It represented the extent to which he and other commanders had embraced Nazi fanaticism and internalised the 'crusading character of the "anti-Bolshevik" war'. What was going on in the last days of Stalingrad was an 'endeavour to stylize the ruin of the Sixth Army, now that it was inevitable, into a historical didactic play about the steadfastness of National Socialist Soldierhood' (Boog et al, p.1163).

Hitler rewarded Paulus for his steadfastness by promoting him to Field Marshal on 31 January. It seems that Hitler hoped that Paulus would do the honourable thing and commit suicide, since no German officer of that high a rank had ever surrendered. That same day, however, Paulus's part in the Stalingrad drama came to an end. Holed up in the *Univermag* Department store in central Stalingrad and surrounded by Soviet troops, Paulus allowed himself to be taken prisoner. In the north of the city General Karl Strecker's 11th Corps held out for a couple more days in the factory district, but that was the end of German resistance in Stalingrad.

Paulus was one of 24 German generals captured at Stalingrad. They were accompanied into captivity by 90,000 other German prisoners, including 2500 officers. The 6th Army, relates Albert Seaton, then began the long march to Soviet prisons in the east of the country:

> 'Time and again the columns were raided for personal belongings, sometimes by Red Army troops but more often by civilians. The prisoners were only lightly guarded but the many men who dropped out through sickness or fatigue were at the mercy of marauding bands of armed civilians who roamed on the outskirts of the columns. None of those who dropped out was ever seen again. Eventually the columns were loaded on to trains and transported through Saratov, Orenburg and Engels to Tashkent, to the north of Afghanistan. At each stop the dead were unloaded from the cattle trucks and only fifty per cent of those who had been entrained arrived at the destination.' (1971, p.336)

It is estimated that only 15,000 of the 90,000 prisoners were still alive by May 1943. Of these only 5000 made it back to Germany after the war, 2000 of them not until 1955. As Seaton indicates the Soviets did not exactly treat the German POWs with kid gloves. Adding to German woes was the fact that the prisoners shared in the hunger experienced by millions of Soviet citizens during the war. But it was the condition of the men when they were captured that accounted for the high rate of attrition, not Soviet maltreatment. Moreover, some categories of prisoner survived better than others. According to Walsh (2000, p.167) while 90 per cent of ordinary soldiers died in captivity, the death rate among junior officers was only 50 per cent and that of senior officers just 5 per cent (Walsh, 2000, p.167). Most of the captured Stalingrad generals survived the war quite well. Many of them, most prominently Seydlitz, emerged as leaders of anti-Nazi organisations of German officers propagandising on behalf of the Soviets. In August 1944 Paulus himself signed an appeal calling for Germans on the Eastern Front to surrender. (It is said that Stalin refused a German offer to exchange Paulus for his son Yakov, a POW who perished in a Nazi prison camp).

The fate of the Stalingrad POWs was an extreme case in terms of their survival rate. Of the 3 million German POWs about two million survived incarceration – a far higher proportion than their Soviet counterparts. Unlike the Germans, the Soviet authorities did not systematically pursue policies that would result in a high death rate among the prisoners it held captive. Indeed, official Soviet policy was that German POWs would be treated in accordance with international law, even though neither Germany nor the USSR were signatories to the relevant treaties and conventions. In practice Soviet treatment of German POWs was much more brutal than it was supposed to be, and on the battlefield Red Army men committed many atrocities against surrendees. One of the worst cases occurred in the Stalingrad theatre in February 1943 when Soviet troops at Krasnoarmeyskoe and Grishno reportedly killed 600

German, Italian, Rumanian and Hungarian POWs and civilian prisoners.

When the battle was all over some 150,000 Germans lay dead in the ashes and rubble of Stalingrad. Total German and Allied casualties resulting from the Stalingrad campaign were in the region of a million and a half. Soviet losses were even greater. The cost was high but, as John Erickson said, when the Red Army encircled the 6th Army at Stalingrad 'the impossible, the unthinkable and unimaginable happened on the Eastern Front' (1983, p.1). The 'impossible, the unthinkable and unimaginable' was victory on such a scale and with such immense consequences.

After Stalingrad, few doubted that the Soviet Union would win the war eventually, not even many Germans.

chapter six

AFTERMATH:

revenge and retribution
on the road to Berlin,
1943 – 5

The Red Army's victorious march to Berlin began with a series of setbacks. In January 1943 the Soviets launched a general offensive in the southern theatre. Building on Operation Little Saturn, the ambitious aim was to entrap, encircle and destroy all the German armies in the south. According to John Erickson 'the Soviet command planned to entomb an estimated seventy-five German divisions in the Ukraine' (1983, p.44).

At first all went well. On 26 January Voronezh was retaken. This was followed by the rout of the Hungarian 2nd Army guarding the Germans' flanks in this sector. On 14 February the Soviets retook Rostov and the next day the Germans evacuated Kharkov. But the Germans had hung on long enough in Rostov to evacuate Army Group A from the Caucasus and in mid-March they were able to launch a counter-attack which recaptured Kharkov (the city changing hands for the third time) from the Soviets. By this time the Soviet counter-offensive was petering out and all operations were grinding to a halt in the spring mud of the *Rasputitsa* ('the time of bad roads'). When the smoke had cleared in spring 1943 the Germans occupied more or less the same positions and front line as they had held in June 1942 on the eve of Operation Blau. After nearly a year of struggle in the south the Germans had gained precisely nothing, at the cost of innumerable armies and divisions, and of a crushing defeat at Stalingrad from which they would never recover.

The main German commander in the south was von Manstein and, thanks mainly to his generalship, the surviving forces of the *Wehrmacht* were able to stage a remarkable defensive recovery and stave off complete disaster in the Stalingrad theatre. Despite the catastrophic defeat at Stalingrad, the *Wehrmacht* remained a formidable fighting force. It was not a force capable any more of winning the war or even of threatening the Soviet strategic position, but it was more than capable of staging a fighting retreat and of inflicting considerable damage on its way back to Germany.

After this post-Stalingrad setback to their grand plans Stalin and the *Stavka* seemed to have finally learned the lesson that the war on the Eastern Front would be won gradually and incrementally rather than by a revolutionary change in the strategic situation. German-style *Blitzkrieg* was abandoned and there was a return to the traditional Soviet doctrine of 'consecutive operations'. Lightning thrusts by armoured formations were not ruled out, but the emphasis was on positional forward movement. Hence, the somewhat surprising Soviet decision to remain on the strategic defensive in 1943, awaiting the Germans' next move, with the intention of anticipating it, defeating it, and using it as a launchpad for a major counter-attack. Again, Zhukov and Vasilevskii were the masterminds of Soviet strategy and tactics.

The German move came at the Battle of Kursk in July 1943. The town of Kursk was near the centre of an outward bulge (a 'salient') in the Soviet defensive line at the junction of the central and southern theatres of operation. The German plan was to pinch out the salient by combined thrusts from Army Group Centre and Army Group South. Soviet forces trapped inside would be encircled and destroyed and the Germans' defensive line could then be shortened and consolidated (see

Map 11, p.xxix). In effect, what the Germans envisaged was a strategic battle of defence, which would inflict great damage on the enemy, regain the initiative in the now crucial central sector, and give themselves some chance of surviving the war on the Eastern Front, for the time being at least. To achieve this result they deployed a huge amount of their remaining armour, including new 'Panther' and 'Tiger' tanks, which outgunned anything the Soviets had in their arsenal.

When the Germans attacked, the Soviets were waiting for them. Kursk was the obvious place for the Germans to make their move, and Stalin had good intelligence on their intentions (including information supplied by western codebreakers) which this time he chose to believe. Defending a series of well-prepared lines, the Red Army absorbed the attempted German panzer *Blitzkrieg*, and then counter-attacked with its own massed armoured formations. At the height of the battle on 11–12 July 1200 tanks met in a single engagement – the greatest such battle of the Second World War. Hour after hour the Soviet and German tank forces pounded each other in a head to head confrontation. Hundreds of tanks were destroyed. Both sides were forced to withdraw. Shortly after, Zhukov visited the scene of the battle and met Soviet tank commander General Nikolai Rotmistrov. Richard Overy describes the scene: 'the two walked out on to the plain, through the corpses and the wrecked machinery of war, the tanks burning fitfully in the summer rain. Zhukov was visibly moved. He removed his cap, and stood for some moments, in thought.' (Overy, 1995, p.95.)

The Germans failed to achieve their objectives at Kursk – they lost heavily in the various engagements that made up the battle, and, within a few weeks, the Soviets had driven the *Wehrmacht* back to the Dnepr River along a broad front, a hundred miles to the west. Before the year was out the Soviets had recaptured Kharkov, Kiev and Smolensk.

Operation Zitadelle (Citadel) at Kursk was the *Wehrmacht*'s last major offensive operation on the Eastern Front. The story of the war thereafter was one of Soviet advances and German retreats. In Soviet legend 1944 became known as the year of the ten great victories:

1. The lifting of the blockade of Leningrad (January).
2. The encirclement of German troops in south-west Ukraine and the Red Army's entry into Rumania (February–March).
3. The liberation of Odessa and the destruction of German forces in the Crimea (April–May).
4. The defeat of Finland at Viborg (which paved the way for the country's surrender in September 1944) (June).
5. The liberation of Belorussia (June).
6. The entry of Soviet forces into Poland (July).
7. The occupation of Rumania and Bulgaria (August).
8. The liberation of Latvia and Estonia (September).
9. The liberation of Belgrade and the entry of Soviet forces into Hungary and Czechoslovakia (October).
10. The defeat of German forces in northern Finland and Northern Norway (October).

(Barber and Harrison, 1991, p.37; Werth, 1964, pp.687–8)

The only hiccup in this continuous Soviet advance was the Red Army's failure to take Warsaw in August 1944. This military failure shortly became a political and human tragedy. When the Red Army reached the Polish capital, the resistance inside the city staged an unsuccessful uprising against the Germans, a move which ended in disaster, and at the cost of 200,000–300,000 lives.

The Warsaw Uprising, staged by Polish nationalists, was very political in intent. They wanted to seize control of Warsaw before the Soviets arrived, thereby gaining a crucial initiative in the looming struggle for the post-war political future of Poland. It was said at the time, and has been said many times since, that the Soviets deliberately and callously stalled their armies on the east bank of the Vistula, just outside Warsaw, which gave the Germans time to finish off the troublesome Polish nationalists who constituted a threat to Soviet post-war control of the country.

However, there were sound military reasons for the Soviet pause before Warsaw. The Red Army had run into stiff German opposition, its supply lines were stretched, and its flanks were vulnerable to counter-attack. The primacy of military, rather than political, motives for the passive Soviet response to the Warsaw Uprising is further attested by the fact that the Red Army was not able to take Warsaw until January 1945 – more than three months after the final failure of the Polish nationalist revolt in September 1944.

This is not to deny that political calculations and prejudices also played their role in Soviet decisions regarding the Warsaw Uprising. Stalin was, indeed, extremely hostile to the Polish nationalists and to the Polish government in exile in

London. The Soviet Union had broken off diplomatic relations with the Polish exile government in 1943 following the infamous 'Katyn' incident, one of the most controversial political episodes of the whole war.

Katyn is a forest near Smolensk. In April 1943 the Germans announced that they had discovered there the bodies of 15,000 Polish officers, shot by the Russians after their capture and imprisonment in September–October 1939. The Soviets angrily denied the accusation and denounced the 'discovery' as a Nazi propaganda ploy. The Polish government in exile, however, long suspicious about the fate of their POWs in Soviet hands, called for an international inquiry to establish the truth. Moscow broke off relations with the London-based Poles, accusing them of being more interested in undermining the Allied war effort than in prosecuting the war against the Germans.

When the Red Army recaptured Smolensk in September 1943 the Soviets conducted their own investigation and announced that the Germans had shot the Polish officers themselves. Some 40 years later documents from the Soviet archives showed that Stalin and the Politburo had ordered the mass executions in March 1940. The reason for this action was as simple as it was brutal: the Polish officers – many with a 'bourgeois' or 'petty-bourgeois' background – were deemed to be counter-revolutionary opponents of the Soviet regime and beyond all hope of political redemption. That was the Soviet way under Stalin; political opponents were executed (or, more usually, imprisoned). The same fate had already befallen hundreds of thousands of Soviet citizens in the 1930s. It was, as the documents chillingly reveal, just a routine Politburo decision. At the same time it should be noted that 100,000 or more Polish POWs survived Soviet captivity; indeed, in 1942–3 70,000–80,000 of them were evacuated from the USSR as part of a Polish army that was to fight on the Italian and other fronts. Another 20,000 Poles fought alongside the Red Army in a Polish Communist People's Army.

It is unlikely that Stalin lost any sleep over the fate of the Warsaw Poles, who rose in revolt not just against the Germans but also against his own post-war designs for a Soviet-dominated Poland. Stalin used the excuse of the military situation as a reason for inaction, but there were many occasions during the war when he was prepared to shed Soviet blood for purely political gains. The most famous example of this was Stalin's response to Allied calls for Red Army military action to relieve pressure on the western front following the German Ardennes offensive in December 1944 ('the Battle of the Bulge'). Stalin, who valued the political goodwill of his western allies, duly obliged and ordered the resumption of Soviet offensive action against Germans on the Eastern Front a few days earlier than planned. In the Warsaw case the military options were more limited, but the Red Army could probably have done more to aid the uprising, notwithstanding its distinctly anti-Soviet character. At the very least, Stalin could have responded sooner to British and American requests for facilities that would allow them to drop supplies to the beleaguered Poles. Stalin argued that air supply was a waste of time since the materials were most likely to fall into German hands, which was true enough. But a dark political malevolence lurked behind Stalin's attitude.

The Red Army crossed the Vistula river in January 1945 and took Warsaw. German forces in the rest of Poland were rapidly expelled (but only at the cost of 500,000 Soviet casualties) and by February the Red Army had crossed into central Germany (East Prussia was already under assault) and were preparing for their final push to Berlin. Nearly five million Soviet soldiers were involved in this final attack on the Reich.

One of the key Soviet commanders in the race to Berlin was Chuikov, who led the 8th Guards Army (formerly the 62nd Army of Stalingrad fame) in the attack on the German capital. In the 1960s he claimed that Berlin could have been taken two or three months earlier than May 1945, when it finally fell. One variation of the Chuikov thesis is that Stalin held up the Soviet advance for political reasons. Stalin met with Churchill and Roosevelt at the Yalta conference in February 1945 and, so the argument goes, did not want to disturb these negotiations about the post-war world by a premature Soviet seizure of Berlin. It is not an interpretation that finds much favour with historians. The evidence shows that the Soviets paused before Berlin for much the same reasons they always suspended or slowed down operations: to deal with logistical problems; to consolidate their forces and positions; and in response to powerful resistance from the Germans, who even at this late stage had not given up the fight.

One thing is certain, however: Stalin and the Soviet leadership were absolutely determined that the Red Army would capture Berlin before the western allies could. In strict military and political terms this was *not* absolutely essential. The Soviets had agreements with the British and Americans which divided Germany into zones of military occupation. Berlin, in the east of Germany, was in the Soviet zone of occupation; and, in any case, it had also been agreed that Berlin would be jointly-occupied by Britain, the US and the USSR, each controlling a sector of the German capital. Since the invasion of France in June 1944 Allied forces had been driving on Germany from the west, and by February 1945 the Allies had crossed the Rhine and were heading for Berlin themselves. It may be that Stalin worried that if the western allies took Berlin they would then renege on their commitments about shared occupation and control of the German capital. But much more important was the psychology and the symbolism involved. As Glantz and House put it:

'Everyone from I.V. Stalin down to the lowest soldier was emotionally and mentally preoccupied with seizing Berlin. After more than three years of enormous destruction and horrendous casualties, the Soviet forces were determined to destroy the enemy regime and bring the war to an end. Moreover, having expended so much blood and energy to defeat the German army in the field, Soviet commanders were in no mood to allow their Western allies to seize the final victory ... this emotional preoccupation drove the Red Army forward to Berlin.' (1995, p.256)

The Soviet assault on Berlin began on 16 April 1945. The German capital was attacked from all directions by a force of more than two million, supported by 6000 tanks, 40,000 artillery pieces and 7500 aircraft. Opposing the Red Army was a motley force of nearly one million Germans with 1500 tanks and 9000 pieces of artillery. Leading the attack was Zhukov, who commanded the armies of the 1st Belorussian Front.

Despite their overwhelming superiority, the Soviets found taking Berlin to be a tough proposition. The battle for Berlin was one of the hardest fought of the Eastern Front campaign and it took the Red Army nearly three weeks of street-to-street and house-to-house fighting to complete their capture of the city. The parallel with Stalingrad was uncanny, except that this was a battle on a much larger scale and was fought for symbolic rather than strategic reasons.

By the end of April Hitler had committed suicide in his Berlin bunker headquarters. The next day, 1 May 1945, the Soviet flag was hoisted on top of the ruined *Reichstag* parliamentary building in the centre of Berlin. Flying the red flag in the enemy's capital on May Day was a fitting political climax to the communist regime's triumph over Nazi Germany. A week later the Germans formally surrendered and the war in Europe was declared to be over.

After the war, the German army's fighting retreat from Russia, and in particular its last-ditch defence of Berlin, were often depicted as heroic struggles, as exemplars of devotion to duty and willing self-sacrifice in the tradition of the 6th Army at Stalingrad. But in their retreat from Russia in 1943–4 the *Wehrmacht* did not give up fighting the war of annihilation they had begun in 1941–2. In mid-1942 a new phase in the ethnic cleansing of Soviet Jewry began and continued for another two years. The retreating

German armies practised a 'scorched earth' policy. Whole cities, towns and villages were razed to the ground. Soviet citizens were deported to Germany as slave labourers in ever-larger numbers. Omer Bartov cites the following example from the record of the 18th Panzer Division's retreat westwards:

> 'In February 1943 . . . the division ordered that all areas about to be given up were to be emptied of their population. Men between the ages of 15 and 65 were to be arrested, all property confiscated and all houses burned down. Similarly, during its retreat from Orel in July and August 1943 [after Kursk], the division evacuated all men of 14–55 and women of 14–45 years old, and established a special 'command', whose duty was to destroy all economic assets in the area, such as machinery, agricultural implements, stocks of crops, windmills, and, of course, to burn down the villages.' (1986, p.146)

As the Soviet partisan struggle in the occupied territories grew, so too did the intensity and ruthlessness of the German reprisal policy. The area of the greatest partisan activity was Belorussia, which suffered 20–25 per cent civilian fatalities during the war. Of the two million civilian dead, 250,000 were killed in anti-partisan operations by the Germans. The rest of the victims were Jews, deportees or other casualties of the war or German occupation.

Overall, there were about 16 million Soviet civilian war deaths. Of these, 11 million died under German occupation and five million were victims of Nazi deportation. It is difficult to be precise about civilian death rates during the period

1941–5, but certainly several million Soviet civilians fell victim to the Germans *after* Stalingrad. As to military casualties, from 1943–5 Red Army losses totalled over 16 million, including four million dead. (Total Soviet military fatalities for the whole war were about eight million.) Some of the hardest battles were on German soil, as the *Wehrmacht* fought ferociously to defend its native land. From January–May 1945, the Red Army suffered well over a million casualties in Germany, including 250,000 dead. The three-week battle for Berlin in April–May 1945 cost nearly 80,000 Soviet lives.

The extent to which Soviet soldiers were personally affected by the German invasion and occupation is shown by the following poll statistics for the 2nd Guards Tank Corps. The fate of the relatives of 5848 servicemen polled was as follows: 4447 killed by the Germans; 1169 maimed; and 908 deported to Germany. The Germans had also burnt down 2430 villages, towns, cities and settlements where the 2nd Guards soldiers had lived before the war (Axell, 2001, p.5). Another example concerns a single Red Army regiment in which 158 of the men had close relatives who had been killed or tortured; the families of 56 of them had been deported; and 445 of the troops knew their homes had been destroyed or ruined (Duffy, 1991, p.273).

As well as nursing their own personal grief and grudges, the Red Army soldiers advancing to Berlin were witnesses to the mass death and devastation caused by the Germans in European Russia. And what they did not witness personally they were informed about by report after report appearing in Soviet newspapers.

In his book, *Russia at War* (1964, pp.551–2), Alexander Werth cites the example of the city of Kharkov, which he visited in February 1943. The grim statistics were as follows. When the German 6th Army took Kharkov in October 1941 the population numbered about 700,000. Fifteen months later half of them had disappeared. According to official Soviet figures (which Werth backs up) 120,000 people were deported to Germany as slaves; 80,000 had died of hunger, cold and deprivation; and 30,000 had been shot.

Another example was the Ukrainian capital Kiev, liberated from the Germans in November 1943. Here the Germans plundered or destroyed 6000 buildings and 1000 factories; killed 200,000 civilians; and deported another 100,000. Overall the city's population was reduced to a fifth of its pre-war size. That is not forgetting Babi Yar, of course (Read and Fisher, 1992, p.153).

Werth also had the doubtful privilege of visiting the Maidanek death camp in Poland shortly after the Red Army 'liberated' it in July 1944. This ghastly scene of the gassing of scores of thousands of Jews and other prisoners was described by Konstantin Simonov and published in *Pravda* and other Soviet newspapers. 'That which I am about to write of is too immense and too frightening to be comprehended in its entirety', he told his readers. Maidanek was the first of many murder factories overrun by the Red Army in German-occupied Poland. Others included Auschwitz, Belzec, Chelmno, Sobibor, and Treblinka – the darkest roll call of horror in the annals of human existence.

All this is indispensable to understanding the storm of retribution and revenge that the Red Army unleashed on Germany and the Germans as it advanced to Berlin in 1945. The Soviets did not exactly pay the Germans back in kind. They committed plenty of atrocities but did not organise systematic mass murder or reprisals of the kind practised by the Germans. There was plunder and pillage aplenty but nothing to match the German destruction of Russia. One of the most typical forms of revenge was the rape of German women.

The extent of the Red Army's mass rape of German girls, women and old ladies is difficult to judge. Even before Soviet forces crossed into Germany, Nazi propagandists were predicting that the Asiatic hordes of judeobolshevism would mass rape German womanhood. After the war wildly exaggerated figures were bandied about as part of an effort to partially exonerate Germany's war record by showing how much the Germans, particularly innocent women and children, had suffered too. Norman Naimark, the author of the most careful summary of the evidence, has this to say:

'It is highly unlikely that historians will ever know how many German women were raped by Soviet soldiers in the months before and the years after the capitulation. It may have been tens of thousands or more likely in the hundreds of thousands. It is even possible that up to 2 million women and girls suffered this crime of violence ...' (1995, p.132–3)

Tens of thousands of rapes would have been 'normal' for such a conquering army, given the scale of the conflict and the size of countries involved. That is probably the kind of tally the

Germans notched up on the Eastern Front, although murder, not rape, was their more typical 'crime of violence'. As it marched its way through Eastern Europe on its way to Germany, the Red Army raped thousands of local women – the number depending on whether the country was being liberated from Nazi rule (Czechoslovakia, Poland, Yugoslavia) or was a conquered Axis state (Rumania, Bulgaria, Hungary). Whether the country was Slavic or not also had an impact. Women in Bulgaria, a Slav state traditionally very close to Russia and a reluctant participant in the Axis, suffered the revenge rape phenomenon hardly at all. In Magyar Hungary it was a different story. But contingent factors were also important. Rape and pillage in Hungary, for example, were exacerbated by the high casualties suffered by the Red Army in capturing Budapest. Bulgaria was also very fortunate to come within the remit of a Soviet commander who maintained the discipline of his troops.

What Soviet soldiers did in Eastern Europe is not surprising. As Susan Brownmiller pointed out in her classic study *Against Our Will* (1975), rape is an established part of warfare. In particular, it is what conquering armies do, to a lesser or greater degree, depending on the circumstances. But hundreds of thousands of rapes in Germany point to a very different scale of the victor rape phenomenon – a mass activity, involving a substantial minority of the Red Army as participants, bystanders or witnesses.

In a particular set of circumstances, conquering soldiers will commit rape for a variety of reasons: because they have been brutalised by war and are inured to human suffering, particularly that of the enemy; because they are drunk, sexually frustrated, and out of control; because they are misogynists who want to exercise power over women; because such violence and the form it takes expresses their male identity; or because rape is another way of striking, indirectly, at the men they are fighting.

Such general factors go some way to explaining the Red Army's assault on German women. But it is also necessary to factor in the Soviet soldiers' particular deep-felt hatred of the Germans and their widespread desire to wreak revenge. Moreover, that hatred and wish for revenge had a crucial, legitimating political context. As the Red Army fought its way west, the anti-German hate propaganda of Ilya Ehrenburg and others continued. When Soviet forces invaded Germany, Ehrenburg announced that the hour of revenge had struck. It was a message hammered home by posters put up in Germany: 'Red Army Soldier: You are now on German soil; the hour of revenge has struck'. About to cross into East Prussia the soldiers of the 3rd Belorussian Front were told by their commanders:

> 'Comrades! You have reached the borders of East Prussia and will now tread on that ground which gave birth to those Fascist monsters who devastated our cities and homes, and slaughtered our sons and daughters, our brothers and sisters, our wives and mothers. The most inveterate of those brigands and Nazis sprang from East Prussia. For many years they have held power in Germany, directing this nation and its foreign aggressions and its genocide of other peoples.' (Duffy, 1991, p.285)

Zhukov's order to the 1st Belorussian Front stated: 'Woe to the land of the murders. We will get our terrible revenge for everything.' Soviet political officers told their men that 'on German soil there is only one master – the Soviet soldier, that he is both the judge and punisher for the torments of his fathers and mothers, for the destroyed cities and villages.' (Naimark, 1995, p.72.)

These official incitements to revenge reflected a hatred of the Germans shared by the top Soviet leadership. One of Stalin's sons was captured by the Germans and died in prison. Throughout the war Stalin was a strong advocate of a punitive peace that would not repeat the allegedly soft treatment of Germany after the First World War. In March 1945 he told a visiting Czechoslovakia delegation in Moscow:

> 'We are now smashing the Germans, and many people assume that the Germans will never be able to threaten us again. Well, that's simply not true. I HATE THE GERMANS! ... It's impossible to destroy the Germans for good ... We are fighting the Germans, and we will finish the job. But we must bear in mind that our allies will try to save the Germans ... We will be merciless towards the Germans, but our allies will seek to treat them more leniently.' (Kramer, 1999, pp.1097–8)

At the same time, it was not open season on the Germans. The Soviet authorities certainly turned a blind eye to sporadic atrocities committed by the Red Army and were indulgent on the rape issue. But there were limits to the indiscipline and violent anarchy they were prepared to accept, particularly when it clashed with other policy goals.

In February 1945 the Soviet Army newspaper *Red Star* warned:

> ' "An eye for an eye, a tooth for a tooth" is an old saying. But it must not be taken literally. If the Germans marauded, and publicly raped our women, it does not mean that we must do the same ... Our revenge is not blind. Our anger is not irrational. In an access of blind rage, one is apt to destroy a factory in conquered enemy territory – a factory that would be of value to us. Such an attitude can only play into the enemy's hands.' (Werth, 1964, p.865)

As this quotation indicates, the official policy of retribution was economically-driven. The Soviet government's priority on invading and occupying Germany was to extract reparations from the country to compensate for the *Wehrmacht*'s devastation of Russia. It is estimated that the Soviets removed at least 25 per cent and perhaps as much as 50 per cent of the industrial capacity of their zone of occupation in Eastern Germany (which, admittedly, was a mainly agricultural region). This included dismantling and shipping to Russia some 4000 factories in 1945 alone. Of growing concern to the Soviet authorities was that the widespread personal pilfering and plundering by its soldiers was hindering the official policy of an organised exploitation of occupied Germany and alienating those elements of the population whose cooperation was needed to achieve this goal.

Shortly after the cautionary *Red Star* article, Moscow signalled a radical change in the policy of wreaking revenge against Germany. In April 1945 an article appeared in *Pravda* attacking Ehrenburg's anti-German hate propaganda and drawing a sharp distinction between Hitler and the Nazis and the general population of Germany. This shift in policy was the public face of the abandonment by Stalin of the project of a punitive peace. All through the war Stalin had advocated the permanent weakening of Germany by its dismemberment – the breaking up of the country into a number of smaller units. In March 1945 that policy was dropped when it became clear that the western allies were more inclined to rehabilitate the Germans than punish them. Stalin now embraced the idea of a cooperative post-war German state, under Soviet influence if not direct control. This new policy necessitated building bridges to the German people, not widening the wartime gulf by excessive acts of revenge. Reinforcing this policy direction were complaints from German political allies of the Soviets who criticised, in particular, the indiscriminate nature of Red Army rapes, whose victims included many communist and anti-Nazi women. As Antony Beevor points out (2002), the Soviet authorities were also aware of reports of Soviet soldiers raping non-German nationals, including many citizens of the USSR forcibly imported into the country as slave labourers during the war.

The new, official policy of restraint and conciliation did not impact greatly on Red Army behaviour, at least when it came to rape. By far the greatest incidence of rape occurred in the greater Berlin area, after the fall of the city in May 1945. And rape, as a widespread phenomenon of the Soviet zone of occupation, continued until the late 1940s. The example of Austria is also interesting in this respect. There was no official incitement of revenge on Austria. On the contrary, Austria, taken over by Hitler in the *Anschluss* of 1938, was depicted in official propaganda as a victim of the Nazis and as a country the Red Army was liberating rather than invading or occupying (except temporarily). Soviet soldiers, however, knew that the Austrians had participated in the war on Russia in as great a number and with as much enthusiasm as other Germans. Many remembered, in particular, that among those who had fought hardest at Stalingrad were the Austrians. There were also a great number of Ukrainians in the Soviet armies which invaded Austria. And if there was any pattern to those that did and those that didn't, it was that Soviet soldiers from territories occupied by the Germans were more likely to commit rape.

Again, the figures are patchy, and probably exaggerated, but it may be that 70,000–100,000 women were raped by the Red Army in Vienna alone. Gunter Bischof concludes that 'undoubtedly the crime of violence against women was as common in Austria as in Germany.' It seems that a particular source of anger for Soviet soldiers in Austria (and the same applied in Germany) was the comparatively high standard of living of the population, even in conditions of wartime. As Bischof notes, there was an element of 'class war' in the revenge visited on the Germans by underprivileged Soviet workers and peasants (1999, pp.30–4).

It should be stressed, however, that rape and other acts of violent revenge were committed by only a minority of the many millions of Soviet soldiers who took part in the invasions of Germany and Austria. Although it should be noted, too, that a much larger number must have looked on, saying and doing nothing to stop what was happening. But as well as the harrowing reports of Red Army brutality towards the German population there is also much evidence of discipline, restraint, and even kindness on the part of many Soviet soldiers.

The Red Army's actions should also be seen in a more general context of revenge and retribution against the Germans at the war's end. Among the millions of POWs and slave labourers in Germany liberated by the Red Army, there were many who played their part in the rape and mayhem. Throughout Eastern Europe, German communities were the objects of violence, terror and intimidation by local populations. Some 13–15 million ethnic Germans were expelled from their traditional homelands in East Prussia, Poland, Russia, Czechoslovakia, Rumania, Hungary, Yugoslavia and the Baltic states. According to one estimate 600,000 were killed by local forces. According to another, two million died as a result of their displacement. The Red Army's revenge on Germany and the Germans seems almost mild by comparison.

As far as the Soviet regime was concerned, revenge and retribution against Germany had a high but not *the* highest priority (except economically). Top of the list was dealing with those Soviet citizens who had collaborated with the Germans. These fell into two main categories. First, nationalities and ethnic groups deemed collectively guilty of collaboration or sympathy for the German invaders. Among the alleged culprits were Volga Germans, Crimean Tatars, Chechens and a number of other peoples from Transcaucasia. Their collective punishment was mass deportation (which began during the war) to Siberia and points east. As many as a million people were so deported. Second, were the estimated one million individual Soviet citizens who fought on the side of the Germans, played a role as auxiliaries (for example, the 'Hiwis') or collaborated in other ways – as bureaucrats, informers, concentration camp staff, and so on. Suspicion also fell on many Soviet POWs, who were seen as not being resolute enough in evading capture or in being prepared to die on the field of battle. The same general attitude applied to the four million or more surviving slave labourers from Soviet territories imported into Germany. In response to this problem the Soviets insisted that all their former citizens should be repatriated, whether they liked it or not. The five to six million returnees were received in dozens of Soviet prison camps and reception centres and their *bona fides* investigated. After the war a quarter of a million people were convicted on various counts of the Soviet equivalent of 'treason' and shot or imprisoned. Many more repatriatees experienced employment discrimination and/or had their rights of abode and movement curtailed. As always in the rigid and unforgiving Soviet system, a good many innocents suffered along with the guilty.

Rape, retribution, revenge, forced repatriation – all this was a very long way from the heroics of Stalingrad and came to cast a long shadow over the Soviet victory in World War II. As Geoffrey Hosking says: 'the war showed the Soviet system at its best and at its worst' (1990, p.295).

When Antony Beevor's *Berlin: The Downfall 1945* was published in 2002, the reviews and press coverage concentrated not on the historical significance of the defeat of the Nazi regime but on the rape issue – the behaviour of the Red Army said by some to symbolise the triumph of an evil, totalitarian Soviet regime. It was a familiar theme in one version of the post-war western narrative of the struggle on the Eastern Front, depicting it as a cruel episode in the history of humanity for which both sides were equally to blame. But this interpretation did not have much credibility at the end of the war, at least not in the Allied world. In 1945 the Red Army was almost universally admired as the saviour of Europe from barbarism. It had fought a savage war against a cruel enemy, and for that most of the world was thankful, if not entirely uncritical. There simply was no gainsaying the sacrifices of the Red Army and the Soviet people. And, above all there was Stalingrad – a story which defied political caricature, manipulation or neutralisation, and which resisted the narrow ideological boundaries of the Cold War era.

chapter seven

THE STALINGRAD STORY:

the battle that history changed, 1945 – 2000

Like all great battles, Stalingrad was destined to be re-fought time and again – in works of history, in memoirs, in fiction and on film. Among the first into the fray were the German generals with memoirs defending their actions on the Eastern Front. The theme of these writings was summed up by the title of von Manstein's memoirs published in 1955: *Lost Victories*. Germany had lost the war, and suffered catastrophe, primarily because of Hitler. The greatest defeat and catastrophe of all was, of course, Stalingrad – a disaster that could have been avoided, or at least minimised, had Hitler followed different advice.

Retired generals excusing their own mistakes and explaining how they would have won the war, was hardly a phenomenon restricted to post-war Germany. More important was how the memoirs of senior commanders like von Manstein harmonised with another strand of the post-war German treatment of Stalingrad: the battle as an example of human folly, trauma and unnecessary sacrifice on a gigantic scale. According to popular historical and fictionalised accounts of Stalingrad, the men of the 6th Army were patriotic heroes misled, betrayed, and forsaken by their leaders. The finger of guilt pointed firmly at Hitler and the Nazis.

In post-war German culture Stalingrad became emblematic of the victimhood of Germany and the Germans at the hands of Hitlerism. Particularly in film and fiction the Second World War was portrayed as a morality play featuring stories of suffering and human tragedy. Stalingrad fitted into this narrative very well. What could be more tragic than the heroic effort and defeat of the 6th Army? The 6th Army's tragedy was all the more poignant because of the fate of many of the survivors of Stalingrad – incarcerated in Soviet camps and prisons for years after the war. Indeed, it was not until 1955 that the last POWs were repatriated to Germany from the Soviet Union.

Alongside this narrative of German victimhood ran an account of the brutality, destructiveness and pathos of war. Again, Stalingrad fitted the bill very neatly. Such imagery was particularly strong in the 1950s when Germans (at least in the western Federal Republic) countered accusations of collective guilt for what had happened during the war with protestations of collective innocence. It was a theme that persisted into the 1990s and beyond. In 1992, for example, Joseph Vilsmaier's feature film *Stalingrad* was released. As a depiction of the harsh and cruel realities of Stalingrad it ranks as one of the greatest ever war films. But politically, ideologically and culturally it stood in a long line of post-war German war films that, as Andreas Kilb, the *Zeit* columnist said, showed the Germans as they most liked to see themselves – as victims of crazed Nazis, the Red Army, the Russian winter, and of a war they never wanted to fight (Moeller, 2001, p.195).

German military commanders did not escape public censure – their leadership and relations with Hitler were questioned, too – but the popular account of the war as tragedy had a major advantage for them: it distracted attention from the character of the annihilatory war waged by Germany on the Eastern Front. As Manfred Messerschmidt relates, in November 1945 a group of leading German generals, including von Manstein, submitted a memorandum to the Allied

International Military Tribunal at Nuremberg denying that the *Wehrmacht* had any responsibility whatsoever for the Nazi exterminationist campaign on the Eastern Front. As Messerschmidt says the claims of the memorandum have no historical merit and do not stand against even a cursory glance at the evidence (Heere and Naumann, 1995, pp.381–99). But the German generals' claims of innocence chimed with the anxieties of the general population, which was also keen to escape any close examination of the war of annihilation. Eighteen million Germans served in the *Wehrmacht* during the war, most of them on the Eastern Front (10 million of them were casualties). Virtually all Germans had an intimate connection with someone complicit with the crimes of the *Wehrmacht*. As we have seen, the other side of the story of the 6th Army's bravery, suffering and devotion to duty at Stalingrad was its prior involvement in the *Vernichtungskrieg*.

In addition to this exculpatory discourse in Germany, there was the effort of professional historians to establish the truth, as they saw it, about Stalingrad. The most effective critiques of the 'blame-it-all-on Hitler' school of thought have been developed by German historians. German historians have contributed greatly to research on the Holocaust and the exterminationist dimensions of the *Wehrmacht*'s Eastern campaign. Above all, German historians have challenged the post-war myths and legends about Stalingrad, exposing the gaps and contradictions in both popular and elite accounts of the battle and of the war in general. At the same time, German social historians influenced by the *Altagsgeschichte* (everyday history) movement have shared with popular history writers a concern to depict battle and war as it was experienced from below, from the point of view of the rank and file as well as officers and the high command.

This combination of dialogue and contradiction between professional history and popular mythologising is a common feature of the universal clash between patriotic defences of national histories and more impartial searches for the truth about the past. This particular case also points to a paradox in the function of the Stalingrad story in post-war western Germany (communist East Germany, which closely followed the Soviet model and pattern of historiography, was another matter altogether). Legends may not be true but they can nevertheless play a positive role. In the case of Germany, the Stalingrad myth was one way of distancing the country and its people from their Nazi past. The victimhood and hon-ourable sacrifice of the 6th Army at Stalingrad was a means of rehabilitation, both in the Germans' own self-image and in the eyes of other western communities. The message was that the Germans were not so bad, after all; they had not all been Nazis; they had shared in a common experience of wartime suffering; and, having atoned for their sins, were now suitable subjects for democratic salvation.

Myths and legends also featured heavily in post-war Soviet accounts of Stalingrad. The Soviet story of Stalingrad, how-ever, was a victor's story, a narrative not of victimhood and tragedy, but of heroism and of triumph over adversity.

For the first decade after the war, accounts of individual and collective bravery in the defence of the city predominated in

Soviet treatments of the battle. At the same time, there was also a more realistic strand in the depictions of the brutal and brutalising human story of the battle, particularly in fictional works by Konstantin Simonov, Vasilii Grossman, Viktor Nekrasov, and others. The war, after all, was a recent memory and for most people was far from being seen as a romantic experience, at least not yet.

In the Soviet Union the historiography of Stalingrad was subject to major ideological and political distortion. The point of departure for this historiography was the wartime myth of Stalin's military genius. After the war Stalin reasserted Communist Party control and sidelined the Soviet military leadership. Zhukov, for example, was demoted and banished to a relatively minor military post in Odessa. During the war Stalin had shared the glory of the victories of Moscow, Stalingrad, Kursk and Berlin with his generals. Now the individual credit was to be his alone.

In the case of Stalingrad, the presentation of Stalin's role had two specific casts. First, that he was the architect of the victorious counter-offensive. This claim went way beyond claiming credit for Operation Uranus and the encirclement of the 6th Army. The whole Stalingrad campaign was presented as a deliberate ploy by Stalin to draw the Germans in and spring a trap to destroy them. In fact, all Soviet defeats and retreats during the war were explained away by reference to Stalin's doctrine of the 'counter-offensive' – all the apparent setbacks were planned, controlled and destined to be victorious. Second, there was the rather more surprising claim that Moscow rather than Stalingrad was the main target of the German summer campaign of 1942. Soviet publicists took their cue on this matter from a statement by Stalin in his Russian Revolution anniversary speech in November 1942:

'What was the principal objective of the German-Fascist strategists when they started their summer offensive on our front? To judge by the comments of the foreign press, including the Germans, one might think that the principal objective of the offensive was to capture the oil districts of Grozny and Baku. But the facts decisively refute this assumption. Facts show that the Germans' advance on the oil districts of the USSR was not their main aim, but an auxiliary one.

What then was the principal objective of the German offensive? It was to outflank Moscow from the east, to cut it off from our rear in the Volga and Urals areas, and then to strike at Moscow. The advance of the Germans southwards towards the oil districts had an auxiliary purpose, which was not only and not so much to capture the oil districts as to divert our main reserves to the south and to weaken the Moscow front, so as to make it easier to achieve success when striking at Moscow ... In short, the main aim of the Germans' summer offensive was to surround Moscow and end the war [in 1942].' (Stalin, 1943, pp.37–8)

Stalin's rationalisation for the holding back of Soviet reserves from the southern theatre was obvious, and he evidently felt the need for this defensive explanation to continue in post-war histories of Stalingrad. It also reveals, perhaps, the extent to which Stalin was wedded to the idea that Moscow (the central theatre) was the key war zone, both at the time and in retrospect. For this reason, while Stalingrad was hailed as a great victory it was not yet presented as the definitive turning point of the war as it was in later Soviet historiography.

After Stalin's death in 1953 Zhukov was rehabilitated and brought back into the leadership fold as defence minister, although he later fell foul of the new Soviet leader, Nikita Khrushchev. At the 20th Congress of the Soviet Communist Party in February 1956 Khrushchev denounced Stalin for his crimes against the Soviet people, for his many political mistakes and for his dictatorial rule over his comrades, including the Politburo and central committee of the Communist Party.

Among other things, Khrushchev's speech opened the floodgates for criticism of Stalin's war leadership. The main focus of the critique was the disaster of the German surprise attack on 22 June 1941, but mistakes in the Stalingrad campaign were also admitted and the ensuing defence of the city was presented more realistically, as not pre-planned but as arising from prior defeats and setbacks. Zhukov and others were rehabilitated and the role of the military as well as political leadership in securing the Soviet victory asserted. By the late 1950s and early 1960s, the first serious and detailed histories of Stalingrad began to appear in the Soviet Union. These, too, were distorted by the exigencies of the current Soviet leadership (there was now a minor cult of Khrushchev's personality), but the new works contained a core of professional research, analysis and argument, much of which still forms the basis for accounts of the battle by western and other authors.

The new historical treatment of Stalingrad was part of a massive expansion of the coverage of the Great Patriotic War in the Soviet Union that developed from the mid-1950s onwards. Post-Stalin, the Soviet victory in that war was a key component of the communist regime's claim to legitimacy, authority and patriotic identity. Stalingrad offered a particularly powerful metaphor legitimising the continuity of communist rule in Russia. Here was a battle which exemplified all the qualities that had won the war and saved the country from complete catastrophe: heroic popular sacrifice; national unity; professional military leadership; communist political mobilisation; and the Soviet system's delivery of the resources and means of victory.

It was not until the 1980s during Gorbachev's *glasnost* era, that the Soviet myths of Stalingrad began to be challenged in the USSR. Revision of the traditional Soviet story continued in the 1990s and has had a number of themes. First, it was increasingly admitted that it was not all heroics at Stalingrad; human weaknesses and fallabilities were present at the battle in large, if not equal, measure. The role of coercion in forcing Soviet soldiers to fight at Stalingrad and elsewhere on the Eastern Front began to be openly discussed for the first time. The 1989 edition of Alexander Samsonov's *Stalingradskaya Bitva* (Stalingrad Battle) which is still the standard Soviet/Russian work on the topic, carried the full text of Stalin's Order 227 of July 1942 detailing coercive measures to ensure that there were no more unauthorised retreats. Allied to these correctives to the official story was a re-assertion of the brutal realities of the battle and of life on the front-line. In this respect there was a significant convergence between

Soviet and German historical discussions of Stalingrad and the Eastern Front war.

Second, there was discussion of Soviet mistakes during the Stalingrad campaign, and not only those of Stalin. The Kharkov disaster of May 1942 came under scrutiny, as did the post-Stalingrad failures of the Red Army. The veracity of Soviet military memoirs was questioned and the issue of the authorship of Operation Uranus re-opened (the controversy about the credit for the counter-offensive plan had begun in the 1960s).

Third, there was a challenge to the very idea that Stalingrad was a test for the Soviet system, which it had passed with flying colours. One variant of this view, common also among western historians, was the argument that Stalingrad was won in spite of the Soviet system, as a result of a combination of patriotism *and* individualism. It was individual initiative, moral autonomy, self-help and responsibility that made possible the overcoming of seemingly insuperable odds of survival and victory at Stalingrad, and in the war generally. None of these personal qualities was conspicuously evident in the Soviet system, except perhaps among its dissidents. A more sophisticated version of this argument points not just to the liberation of the spirit of the Soviet people during the war, but also to the transformation of the Soviet system symbolised by what happened at Stalingrad. This is the theme of Vasilii Grossman's novel of the war *Zhizn' i Sud'ba* (Life and Fate), written in the 1950s but not published until 1988. A Soviet reviewer of the book had this to say of Grossman's text:

'Stalingrad is the crisis point of the war ... On the one hand Stalingrad is the spirit of freedom and the spirit of liberation. On the other hand it is the symbol of the Stalin system, which is hostile to freedom in its very essence.... Stalingrad in *Life and Fate* is both an heroic act and the tragedy of a people which, liberating itself, liberating the country and liberating the world from fascism, simultaneously also liberated Stalin. It liberated Stalin from his past ... "He knew better than anyone else in the world", Grossman writes about Stalin, "that victors are not judged" .... "The victory at Stalingrad", we read in the novel, "determined the outcome of the war, but the silent quarrel between the victorious people and the victorious state continued".' (Davies, 1989, pp.110–11)

Grossman's view of the liberating, individualistic dimension of the Soviet war effort was probably over-romantic. During the war the Communist Party continued to play its key organisational and mobilisational role in Soviet society. In many ways the war strengthened communist legitimacy and authority, while enabling other actors and institutions, such as the military, to come to the fore. During the war there were three million communists – half the party's membership – serving in the armed forces. Moreover, as Robert Service points out, the patronage and clientelism of the infrastructure of the Soviet regime in the 1920s and 1930s, often revolving around party institutions and power networks, was very much alive during wartime (1997, p.278).

Still, it could be argued that the victory at Stalingrad pointed in many directions. One was towards a post-war reform of Soviet society which would not threaten Stalin and the communist system but which could build on the foundation of the greater flexibility and freedom (within limits) of the system during wartime. As in the case of West Germany, the Stalingrad myth might have been utilised for the purposes of progress towards a more liberal and tolerant society. The 'silent quarrel' between state and society could have been resolved by a new compact – such a compact would both recognise the sacrifices and needs of the people, while acknowledging the legitimacy of a system which had proved itself in wartime, at least to a degree. In one sense this is what began to happen in the Soviet Union in the 1950s and 1960s, finally coming to fruition (briefly) in the 1980s under Gorbachev. In the immediate post-war period, however, there was a reversion to rigid Stalinism. One of the main reasons this happened was the outbreak of the Cold War in 1947–8. The Cold War was initially a series of quarrels between the members of the victorious wartime coalition over differences about the kind of peace that would best suit the conflicting interests and ideologies of the Allies. From this beginning the Cold War rapidly grew into a split between competing military-political blocs in Europe and in the global arena. For Stalin and the Soviet Communist Party the Cold War context provided a ready-made rationalisation for orthodoxy and repression at home, running in parallel with conflict and confrontation abroad.

The Cold War had its impact, too, on the treatment of Stalingrad in the western historiography of the Second World War. During and immediately after the war the battle loomed large as the great turning point in the chain of events from 1939–45. Naturally, different countries highlighted different landmarks of the wartime landscape. For the British there was Dunkirk, the Battle of Britain, El Alamein and D-Day. For Americans there was Pearl Harbour, Midway, D-Day, and the dropping of atomic bombs on Japan. For the French the fall of France in 1940 and its liberation in 1944 were the crucial events. But there was also a shared sense of proportion cutting across national boundaries when it came to comparisons with the significantly larger scale and importance of the decisive battles on the Eastern Front, particularly Stalingrad. After all, it was Churchill who had said during the war that it was the Red Army which tore the guts out of Hitler's war machine.

Acknowledging the centrality of the German-Soviet struggle to the outcome of the Second World War did not, however, suit the Cold War climate. Instead the western Cold War view stressed the similarities between the dictatorial communist and Nazi systems. That stance could be easily assimilated into a traditional anti-communism which relished the war between two totalitarian regimes as a mutually murderous slugging match. Such had been the fantasy of many conservatives and right-wingers in the 1930s. But in the 1940s and 1950s that stance might have seemed a bit ungrateful, given the millions of Soviet citizens who had died to stop Hitler, who had posed a threat to everyone, not only the communists. Far better simply to ignore or marginalise the Soviet role in the war and to construct a narrative which instead stressed the primacy of the western contribution and perspective on the war. The highpoints of this story of the Second

World War were: the British and French declarations of war
when Germany attacked Poland in 1939, the USSR standing
aside and embracing Hitler in the Nazi-Soviet Pact; the fall
of France in 1940; the Battle of Britain; the US entry into the
war in December 1941; the Battle of the Atlantic and the
Anglo-American air bombardment of Germany; the turning
point of Midway, El Alamein and (*sotto voce*) Stalingrad in
1942; the allied invasions of North Africa, Sicily and Italy in
1942–3; the invasion of France in 1944; the crossing of the
Rhine in February 1945; and the Japanese surrender in
August 1945.

The exclusion of Stalingrad and the Eastern Front from the
western narrative of the war was reflected in the feature films
of the post-war period. A rare exception was Sam Pekinpah's
Cross of Iron, released in 1977, but this treated the Eastern
Front campaign purely from the German point of view (and
the same was true of German-made war films). Stalingrad was
an obvious backdrop for the action and heroics typical of war
movies, but not until the release of *Enemy at the Gates* in
2001 did it get the Hollywood treatment (for which we
should, perhaps, be thankful!).

An important text in the western post-war narrative of the
Second World War was Winston Churchill's multi-volume
memoir-history of the war published during the late 1940s
and early 1950s. As Chuikov later complained: 'in the 4700
pages of his six-volume memoirs ... he devotes less than a
hundred pages to the Soviet-German front, and he distorts
the events that took place there.' (Chuikov, 1963, p.361.)
Stalingrad itself merits barely half a dozen pages, although

Churchill does acknowledge 'the magnificent struggle and decisive victory of the Russian armies' which was a 'crushing disaster ... end[ing] Hitler's prodigious effort to conquer Russia by force of arms and destroy Communism by an equally odious form of totalitarian tyranny.' (Churchill, 1951, pp.571–1)

To an extent the imbalance in Churchill's 'history' was personal and idiosyncratic. As A.J. Balfour famously said of Churchill's account of the First World War: 'I hear that Winston has written a big book about himself and called it *The World Crisis*!' But Churchill's minimalist treatment of the Eastern Front was replicated in many other textbooks and general histories of the Second World War from the 1950s onwards. It was only in the post-Cold War 1990s that this distorted balance began to be corrected and the Eastern Front given the treatment and importance it merited. For example, Gerhard Weinberg's *A World at Arms: A Global History of World War II*, published in 1994, paid far more attention to the Eastern campaign than many of its predecessors. The 1990s were also a time of many television documentaries and series focusing on the Soviet-German war; it was a time, indeed, of great discovery and rediscovery of the 'unknown war' on the Eastern Front.

But all through the cold war the lure of Stalingrad remained. It was just too good a story to ignore; so obviously a tale that was too important to be caricatured and dismissed as simply another barbaric episode in the clash between Nazi and Soviet totalitarianisms. Publications and discussions in Germany and the Soviet Union had an impact and, from the late 1950s, many English-language studies of Stalingrad were published. In addition, there appeared some substantial general accounts of the Soviet-German War – by Alexander Werth (1964), Alan Clark (1965) and Albert Seaton (1971) – which situated the great battle in its wider context. On television the most riveting episodes of the highly acclaimed series, *The World at War*, were about Stalingrad and the Eastern Front. In the 1980s, and particularly the 1990s, they were some notable successors to the histories and documentaries of the 1960s and 1970s, most notably the TV series and book *Russia's War* (see Overy, 1997).

As this book has emphasised already, even while the war was still being fought, the events at Stalingrad played a central role in shaping contemporary perceptions and understandings of the unfolding drama of the great global conflict. By the turn of the century, Stalingrad had resumed its place as a defining battle not just of the Second World War, but of a whole epoch.

chapter eight

CONCLUSION:

the battle that changed history?

So how important was the Battle of Stalingrad to the outcome of the Second World War?

The contemporary verdict was clear. Stalingrad was *the* turning point of the war. After Stalingrad the final defeat of the Axis powers was certain and the ultimate victory of the Allied states was assured. While the battle raged the most frequently-quoted analogy was that of the French defence of Verdun in 1916. After the Soviet victory the reference point shifted to 1918 and to Operation Michael – the last German offensive of the First World War. One variation on this theme was Barnet Nover's comment in an article entitled 'Echoes of Doom', published in *The Washington Post* on 2 February 1943: 'Stalingrad's role in this war was that of the Battle of the Marne [1914], Verdun [1916] and the Second Marne [1918] rolled into one.'

In May 1944 President Roosevelt presented a 'scroll' from the people of the United States to the city of Stalingrad:

'To commemorate our admiration for its gallant defenders whose courage, fortitude, and devotion during the siege ... will inspire forever the hearts of all free people. Their glorious victory stemmed the tide of invasion and marked the turning point in the war of the Allied Nations against the forces of aggression.'

Churchill had delivered his tribute at the Teheran Conference of the top Allied leaders in November 1943, when he presented to Stalin the honorary 'Sword of Stalingrad' – a gift from King George VI and the British people. Stalin kissed the sword and passed it to one of his marshals for safekeeping.

Stalin's own verdict on the significance of the battle was more restrained, however. In a speech on the 26th anniversary of the Russian Revolution in November 1943 he gave equal billing to Kursk as the turning point of the war: 'While the battle of Stalingrad heralded the decline of the German-Fascist army, the battle of Kursk confronted it with disaster.' It was a comment which reflected the Soviet leadership's continuing obsession with the central sector in front of Moscow as the decisive site of battle.

Of course, not everyone saw Stalingrad as the defining moment of German defeat, which augured Soviet and Allied victory in the war. Hitler and his entourage continued to hope that their misfortunes could be reversed and the situation salvaged, a view shared by the more fanatical Nazi element among the German population. But even in Germany the predominant view was that Stalingrad was an unmitigated disaster that marked the turning point from victory to defeat.

After the war the concept of the Stalingrad turning-point dominated much of the historical literature. In a section entitled 'The Importance of the Victory at Stalingrad' in his history of the Second World War, Henri Michel denoted the battle as the 'most crucial victory' of the war (1975, pp.416–18). The Red Army had taken on the full power of the *Wehrmacht* and won, he argued. Michel emphasised, in particular, the political and diplomatic importance of the Stalingrad result. After Stalingrad, Germany's Axis alliance in Europe began to disintegrate. Finland, Hungary and Rumania all began to distance themselves from Germany and to seek a separate peace with the Allies. Like Hungary and Rumania, the Italians lost an army as a result of Stalingrad. This disaster, together with Italian defeats in North Africa in 1942, contributed greatly to Mussolini's woes. He was toppled in a coup in July 1943 and, by September that year, Italy (or at least the part not occupied by the Germans) was fighting on the side of the Allies. Neutral states such as Spain, Sweden and Turkey, which until the Stalingrad defeat had been friendly or cooperative with Germany, began to adopt a more pro-Allied policy. Of particular importance was the position of Turkey. Before Stalingrad (but not after) there was some doubt as to whether Turkey would side with Germany and join in an anti-Soviet campaign – an intervention which could have made a crucial difference to the Russian position in the Caucasus (and also to the British position in the Middle East).

The Soviet victory at Stalingrad also had a considerable impact on the USSR's western allies. After Stalingrad the British and Americans had to reckon with a war that would be won largely by the Soviet Union – a power that would be in a position to dominate post-war Europe. Thus, from 1943 onwards, there were significant moves to enlist the Soviet Union in a grand alliance devoted to the collective organis-ation of the peace and the post-war settlement. From those wartime discussions and negotiations emerged the shape of the post-war political order in Europe.

For post-war military historians the importance of Stalingrad lay in the damage inflicted on the *Wehrmacht*. During the

Stalingrad campaign the Germans suffered more casualties and equipment losses than they had during Barbarossa in 1941, and by 1943 they were in no position to make up the deficit in men and machines. Notwithstanding the German shift to a total war economy after the Stalingrad defeat, the *Wehrmacht* was never again in a position to conduct a strategic campaign on the Eastern Front. The Soviet enemy, on the other hand, went from strength to strength.

For the German military leadership Stalingrad was a moment of major crisis as relations between Hitler and his generals deteriorated and became even less professional than before. Hitler himself was thoroughly shaken by the defeat and did not recover his personal composure for the remainder of the war. Adding to Hitler's troubles was the incentive Stalingrad provided to German military and political conspirators plotting his downfall. In July 1944 the plotters almost succeeded in blowing him up at his military headquarters in East Prussia.

For the Soviets, Stalingrad was the making of a unified military-political leadership that committed fewer and fewer errors as the war progressed. In the longer term, Stalingrad was one of the most important linchpins of the post-war re-foundation of the Soviet regime on foot of victory in the Great Patriotic War. Many people cite Stalingrad as the beginning of the Soviet rise to super-power status. Equally important was the internal cohesion that Stalingrad helped create, by no means complete and conflict free, but sufficient to enable the Soviet state to survive for another 50 years.

On the psychological front, everyone agrees that Stalingrad

was a shattering blow to German and Axis morale and a tremendous boost to the confidence of the Soviets and their Allies. As Richard Overy has noted, the self-belief of the Allied side was always strong; after Stalingrad the certainty of victory was unshakeable – and rightly so.

However, this consensus on the central importance of Stalingrad to the outcome of the war has been challenged from a number of points of view. First, there are those who argue for assigning greater importance to other great battles on the Eastern Front, especially Moscow and Kursk. The argument in favour of Moscow is that if the Germans had captured the Soviet capital in 1941 the Stalin regime would have crumbled. This assessment of the importance of holding on to Moscow is probably correct and underlines how critical it was for the Soviets to win this first big battle. Moscow, however, was a defensive victory for the Soviets which enabled them to live and fight another day. It averted defeat but did not, and could not, guarantee victory. For the Germans it was a big setback but one that did not end their chances of winning the war in the east. They had failed to take Moscow but they had won a springboard in the southern theatre for their Stalingrad campaign. Arguably, the Barbarossa *Blitzkrieg* had failed when the operation stalled at Smolensk in mid-July 1941, long before the Germans reached the outskirts of Moscow. That delay meant a long war of attrition had to be conducted and won on the Eastern Front. The crucial battle in this regard was to be waged at Stalingrad in 1942.

The argument in favour of Kursk is that, while Stalingrad signified that the Germans could never win the war, the Kursk victory guaranteed that the Soviets would win the war, sooner or later. This, indeed, was Stalin's take on the two battles at the time, although later the pre-eminence of Stalingrad came to dominate the Soviet view of the war. The detailed, pro-Kursk argument focuses on the strategic importance of smashing the last major reserves of German armour in summer 1943 and on the fact that, after this defeat, the *Wehrmacht* had no means of seizing the initiative on the Eastern Front. However, Kursk was primarily a defensive battle for both sides. It is difficult to see that it would have made any fundamental difference to the overall strategic position had the Germans won. No doubt success at Kursk would have been a great boost to the *Wehrmacht* and a bitter blow to the Red Army, but the Soviets had already suffered and survived greater defeats in the war and they would have undoubtedly recovered from this one. Soviet survival following a defeat at Stalingrad is not such a self-evident proposition. The resources for recovery would have been available but what about morale? And could the Soviet state have survived such a setback politically? Finally, there is an obvious point to be made about Kursk. As great and important a battle as it was, it came after and on the back of the victory at Stalingrad. No Stalingrad, no Kursk; it's as simple as that.

The Russians distinguish between *povorot* (a turning point) and *perelom* (a breaking point). Moscow and Kursk were undoubtedly great turning points in the war on the Eastern Front, but Stalingrad was also the breaking point, the point of crisis and of radical transformation in the strategic situation. Without the *povorot* of Moscow, no *perelom* at Stalingrad, and no *perelom* at Stalingrad, no *povorot* at Kursk.

Collectively, the battles of Moscow, Stalingrad and Kursk determined the outcome of the Soviet-German conflict and hence the outcome of the Second World War as a whole. This final point is worth underlining again: by far the greatest amount of fighting and numbers of casualties took place on the Eastern Front. It was the epicentre of the global conflict; matchless in the forces mobilised, deployed and committed to battle. Other theatres of war played their part in determining the overall outcome, but they were sideshows in comparison with the struggle on the Eastern Front. The most important contribution made by the western Allies to the war after June 1941 was, arguably, their material aid to the USSR.

A second, more radical position in the debate about the pivotal importance of Stalingrad is one which questions whether which side won the battle was really that important at all. What if the Germans had won at Stalingrad? Given that the German victory could only have been won at great cost, would the *Wehrmacht* have been able to successfully defend from Soviet counter-attack their positions in Stalingrad, and along the Don and Volga? It is an interesting question for war games experts, but highly speculative, and ultimately unanswerable. The Germans certainly thought they could hold the defensive line once it was established (albeit based on their under-estimates of Soviet strength and reserves) and they would surely have been in a much stronger defensive position after a victory at Stalingrad than the one they found themselves in following the encirclement of the 6th Army. Issues of morale and momentum would also have played a crucial role in determining the outcome of a *German* defence of Stalingrad. Moreover, the Germans were not without reserves and resources with which to defend their positions. Even after the massive defeat at Stalingrad von Manstein was able to mobilise and manoeuvre sufficient German forces in southern Russia to halt the follow-on Soviet offensive and to inflict some significant local defeats on the Red Army.

A variation on this challenge focuses on strategic rather than tactical or operational issues. Operation Blau was launched to seize control of vital raw materials, with the oil of Baku as the ultimate prize. Would German seizure of the oil of the Caucasus have made a great deal of difference? In the short term, it is suggested, the Soviets could have fallen back on significant stockpiles of fuel in central and northern Russia, while it would have taken some time for the Germans to repair and make productive the captured oil fields, whose infrastructure the Russians would certainly have destroyed before retreating. In the medium term, the loss of Baku would probably have crippled the Soviet war economy, but by that time, it is argued, the overwhelming material superiority of the Allied side as a whole would have been brought to bear on Nazi Germany.

On the basis of available evidence, it is difficult to assess the short and medium-term impact on the Soviet war economy of a defeat in the southern campaign. Certainly at the time both the Germans and the Soviets foresaw radical consequences arising from Baku changing hands, which is one reason why the two sides fought so hard for victory at Stalingrad and in the Caucasus. As it turned out, the Germans did not need the Caucasus oil as much as they thought they did. Supplies from Rumania and other sources were sufficient to meet most of their needs (until the British and Americans bombed, and then the Soviets overran, the Ploesti fields in 1944).

But beyond short and medium-term issues of oil supply, at stake in the southern campaign was something much more fundamental – Germany's capacity to fight a long global war of attrition against the Soviet Union and its western allies. To do that Germany needed, first, to cripple the Soviet enemy – the force that posed the immediate threat to German power in Europe – and, second, to take control of the resources necessary for long term survival in a global conflict with the British and Americans as well as the Russians. This was the real strategic importance of the battle for Stalingrad and the Caucasus. It was a struggle, not about immediate victory in the war but about continuing the war indefinitely.

But perhaps the truth is that no single battle mattered that much in the end. This is the argument put forward by those who say that what was decisive in the Second World War were economics, industrial power and armaments production. One variation of this argument used to be promulgated by Soviet authors who stressed the superiority of the socialist system and the historical inevitability of the USSR's victory over Nazi Germany. Another variation poses the argument in the context of the global balance of forces between the Allies and the Axis. The Allies won, it is said, because of their superiority in men and matériel. Hitler's only hope of winning was through *Blitzkrieg* and tactical victories to establish an unassailable position for Germany before the economic and industrial power of the Allies, particularly the Americans, was brought to bear. Still others, for example, Alan J. Levine (1985), argue that World War II was never really a near-run thing because detailed examination of German defeats at Stalingrad and elsewhere shows that even Axis victories would not have made much difference in the long run.

The importance of the productive power of the Soviet-Western alliance is beyond doubt, but as Richard Overy says in response to this kind of argument: 'the Allies won the Second World War because they turned their economic strength into effective fighting power, and turned the moral energies of their people into an effective will to win.' (1995, p.325.)

This general point applies in the case of Stalingrad. The Soviets had the resources, forces and will to avert defeat and win, but that did not guarantee victory. Moreover, as Overy also says, 'battles are not pre-ordained. If they were, no one would bother to fight them ... The Battle of Stalingrad depended on the desperate, almost incomprehensible courage of a few thousand men who held up the German 6th army long enough to spring a decisive trap.' (ibid., p.320)

On the other hand, Mark Harrison (2002) points out that, in order to win wars, countries have to solve their moral, technical, political and organisational problems, and these problems are always much easier to solve if the resources are available and favourable. At the time of Stalingrad, however, the balance of resources was by no means uniformly favourable to the Soviet Union. Indeed, as Harrison says,

German victories and occupation of Soviet territory in 1942 had brought the USSR's economy to the point of collapse, to a 'knife-edge'. The victory at Stalingrad – a triumph for Soviet military and political mobilisation – tipped the balance one way, rather than another. But, as the story of Stalingrad shows, different decisions and actions could easily have tipped the balance the other way.

From the point of view of German failure, as opposed to Soviet success, a useful way of thinking about the significance of Stalingrad is that proposed by Bernd Wegner, author of the most comprehensive study of German strategy in 1942. For the Germans, Stalingrad was not so much a turning-point as a 'point of no return'. Stalingrad, as Wegner argues, was:

> 'The final conclusion of a process of diminishing options of victory in the east. The crucial stations of this process were the battle of Smolensk in July 1941 and the resulting stoppage of the German advance, the failure before Moscow in December 1941, the relocation of substantial sections of Soviet industry ... and Hitler's decision in July 1942 to split Operation Blue in two. After each of these events the foundations of a German victory in the east had become more fragile, and the number of options smaller. In this process of a cumulatively progressing turning-point the tragedy of Stalingrad represented the final military consequence. After it there was no realistic hope left of a victory in the east.' (Boog et al, 2001, p. 1214)

Battles do change the course of history. They determine the outcome of wars, the shape and character of victory and the peace that follows. They also change how the history of a war is viewed. In both these respects no battle changed history more than Stalingrad.

Stalingrad was a classic confrontation – a battle of resources, strategy and political will between immensely powerful and equally determined forces. The winner was the side that, in the end, was able to deploy its forces and adapt to the circumstances of the battle most effectively.

The Second World War, whose outcome Stalingrad did so much to determine, concluded with the dropping of atomic bombs on Hiroshima and Nagasaki in August 1945. The coming of the nuclear era meant that there would never be another battle like Stalingrad. The greatest battle of the last great war of the pre-atomic age was an epic struggle that will never be surpassed.

APPENDIX

DOCUMENT 1: STAVKA ORDER NO. 270

ORDER No.270
HEADQUARTERS OF THE SUPREME COMMAND
OF THE RED ARMY
16 AUGUST 1941

Concerning Cowardice and Surrender to Captivity and Measures to Curtail Such Actions

Not only do our friends recognise, but our enemies are forced to acknowledge, that in our liberation war with the German-Fascist invaders the great mass of the Red Army, especially its commanders and commissars, are conducting themselves irreproachably, steadfastly and, at times, heroically. Even those units of the army which find themselves cut off and surrounded maintain their morale and steadfastness, do not surrender to captivity, endeavour to inflict more damage on the enemy, and evade encirclement. As is well known, isolated units of our army, on finding themselves surrounded by the enemy, use every possibility to inflict defeat on the enemy and to escape encirclement.

Deputy Commander of the troops of the Western Front Lieutenant-General Boldin, while in the area of the 10th Army near Belostok and surround by German troops, organised detachments of the Red Army remaining in the rear of the enemy to fight from behind for 45 days and to break through to the main forces of the Western Front. They destroyed the headquarters of two regiments, 26 tanks, 1049 armoured vehicles, transports and staff cars, 147 motorcycles,

5 batteries of artillery, 4 mortars, 15 heavy machine guns, 5 machine-gun platoons, 1 plane at an aerodrome and a store of aviation bombs. Over a thousand German soldiers and officers were killed. On 11 August Lieutenant-General Boldin attacked the Germans from the rear, broke through the German front, and, reuniting with our forces, lead out of military encirclement 1654 Red Army men and their commander, 103 of which were wounded.

The commissar of the 8th Mechanised Corps, Brigade Commissar Popel', and commander of the 406 rifle regiment, Colonel Novikov, led the fight of 1778 people from military encirclement. In persistent battle with the Germans the Novikov-Popel' group traversed 650 kilometres, inflicting enormous losses on the enemy's rear.

Commander of the 3rd Army, Lieutenant-General Kuznetsov, and member of the military council, Army Commissar 2nd Class Birukov, led the fight out of encirclement of 498 armed Red Army men and commanders of the 3rd Army and organised the exit from encirclement of the 108th and 64th rifle divisions.

All these and numerous similar incidents demonstrate the determination of our troops, and the high morale of our soldiers, commanders and commissars.

But we cannot conceal the fact that in the recent period there has taken place several shameful cases of surrender to enemy captivity. Individual generals have given a bad example to our troops.

The commander of the 28th Army, Lieutenant-General Kachalov, together with his staff, found himself surrounded and displayed cowardice and surrendered to German fascist captivity. Kachalov's staff fought their way out of encirclement, along with parts of the Kachalov group, but Lieutenant-General Kachalov preferred to surrender to captivity, preferred to desert to the enemy.

Lieutenant-General Ponedelin, commander of the 12th Army, surrounded by the enemy, had every opportunity to break out, as did the great majority of his army. But Ponedelin did not display the necessary determination and will to victory, yielded to panic and cowardice and surrendered to enemy captivity – deserted to the enemy, thus committing a crime against the motherland as a violator of his military oath.

Surrounded by German-Fascist forces, the commander of the 13th Rifle Corps, Major-General Kirillov, instead of carrying out his duty to his motherland and organising the units entrusted to him to repulse the enemy and escape from encirclement, deserted from the field of battle and surrendered to enemy captivity. As a result, units of the 13th Rifle corps were destroyed, and some of them surrendered to enemy captivity without serious resistance.

It should be noted that in the face of all the indicators of surrender to enemy captivity, members of the military councils, commanders, political workers, and special forces (*'osobootdel'shchiki'*) in the areas of encirclement, demonstrated unacceptable confusion and shameful cowardice and made no effort even to prevent the surrender to enemy captivity of frightened Kachalov, Kirillov and others.

These disgraceful instances of surrender to our sworn enemy are evidence that in the ranks of the Red Army stand not only selfless, wholehearted defenders of their Soviet motherland from invasion, but also unstable, faint-hearted, cowardly elements. And these elements are not only in the ranks of the Red Army but among its command structures. It is well-known that some commanders and political workers in their behaviour at the front are not a model of courage, steadfastness and love for country for Red Army soldiers, but, on the contrary, hide themselves in the trenches, busy themselves with paperwork, not seeing or observing the field of battle, and in the face of the first serious difficulties in battle give in to the enemy, tear off their badges of rank and desert from the field of battle.

Is it possible to tolerate in the ranks of the Red Army cowards, deserting to the enemy and surrendering to captivity, or faint-hearted commanders, who at the first hitch at the front tear off their insignia and desert to the rear? No. It is impossible! If we give in to these cowards and deserters, they will shortly demoralise our army and ruin our country. Cowards and deserters must be eliminated.

Is it possible to regard as commanders of battalions or regiments those battalion and regimental commanders, who think of themselves as commanders, yet who hide in the trenches during battle, not seeing the field of battle or observing the progress of the battle? No, it is impossible! These are impostors, not commanders of battalions and regiments. If we give in to such impostors, they will in a short time turn our army into a massive bureaucracy. It is necessary to quickly remove from their posts such impostors, to demote them, to transfer them to the ranks, to execute them on the spot if necessary, and to replace them with courageous and steadfast people from the ranks of junior officers or Red Army soldiers.

ORDERS

1. Commanders and political workers who during battle tear off their badges of rank and desert to the rear or surrender to enemy captivity, will be considered deliberate deserters, whose families will be liable to arrest as relatives of violators of their oath, traitors and deserters of their country.

    The duty of all higher commanders and commissars is to execute on the spot such deserters among officers.

2. Units and elements finding themselves in enemy encirclement should selflessly fight to the last, guarding equipment with their lives, attack enemy forces from the rear and inflict defeat on the fascist dogs.

    The responsibility of every soldier if his unit is surrounded, irrespective of his official position, is to demand from higher officers to fight to the last and to break out of encirclement. And if officers or soldiers instead of organising a repulse of the enemy prefer to surrender to captivity – destroy them with all means, ground and air.

The families of Red Army men surrendering to captivity will be deprived of state entitlements and assistance.

3. The responsibility of all divisional commanders and commissars is to immediately remove from post battalion and regimental commanders who hide in the trenches during battle, afraid of giving leadership on the field of battle, and to demote such officials as impostors, transfer them to the ranks and if necessary execute them on the spot, promoting in their place courageous and steadfast people from junior officers or from the ranks of outstanding Red Army soldiers.

The order to be read in all companies, troops, squadrons, batteries, commands and staffs.

HEADQUARTERS OF THE SUPREME COMMAND

Chairman of the State Defence Committee	I. Stalin
Deputy Chairman of the State Defence Committee	V. Molotov
Marshal of the Soviet Union	S. Budennyi
Marshal of the Soviet Union	K. Voroshilov
Marshal of the Soviet Union	S. Timoshenko
Marshal of the Soviet Union	B. Shaposhnikov
General of the Army	G. Zhukov

DOCUMENT 2: STALIN ORDER NO. 227 ('NOT A STEP BACK')

ORDER No.227
PEOPLE'S COMMISSAR FOR DEFENCE
28 JULY 1942

The enemy throws at the front new forces and, big losses notwithstanding, is penetrating deep into the Soviet Union, invading new regions, devastating and destroying our towns and villages, violating, robbing and killing the Soviet people. The battle rages in the area of Voronezh, in the Don, in the south at the gateway to the Northern Caucasus. The German occupiers are breaking through towards Stalingrad, towards the Volga and want at any price to seize the Kuban and the Northern Caucasus and their oil and bread resources. The Germans had already taken Voroshilovgrad, Starobel'sk, Rossosh', Kupyansk, Valuiki, Novocherkassk, Rostov-on-Don, and half of Voronezh. Units of the Southern Front, succumbing to panic, abandoned Rostov and Novocherkassk without serious opposition and without orders from Moscow, thereby covering their banners with shame.

The people of our country, for all their love and respect for the Red Army, are beginning to be disappointed by it, are losing faith in the Red Army, and many of them are cursing the Red Army for giving our people over to the yoke of the German oppressors, while itself escaping to the east.

Some silly people at the front comfort themselves by saying that we can retreat further east, that we have much territory, many lands, lots of people and that we will always have plenty of bread. With this they excuse their shameful conduct on the front. But, through falsehoods and lies, such talk helps our enemies.

Every commander, soldier and political worker must understand that our resources are not unlimited. The territory of the Soviet state is not an empty desert but people – workers, peasants, the intelligentsia, our fathers, mothers, wives, brothers and children. The territory of the Soviet Union, which the enemy has seized, or is striving to seize, is bread and other products for the army and the rear, metal and fuel for industry, factories, enterprises, the railways, and supplies for the armed forces and its reserves. After the loss of the Ukraine, Belorussia, the Baltic Republics, the Donbass and other areas we have much less territory, much less metal, much less bread, and many fewer people, factories and enterprises. We have lost more than 70 million in population, and more than 8,000 million puds of bread a year and more than 10 million tons of metal a year. We no longer have more people reserves than the Germans, nor any reserves of bread. To retreat further would mean the ruination of our country and ourselves. Every new scrap of territory we lose will significantly strengthen the enemy and severely weaken our defence, our motherland.

It is necessary, therefore, to stop all talk that we have the possibility of unlimited retreat, that we have a lot of territory, that our country is big and rich, with many people, and bread in abundance. Such talk is lying and harmful, it weakens us and strengthens the enemy, because if there is no end to the retreat, we will be left with no bread, no fuel, no metals, no raw materials, no enterprises, no factories, and no railways.

It follows from this that it is time to finish with retreat.

Not a step back! This must now be our chief slogan.

It is necessary to defend to the last drop of blood every position, every metre of Soviet territory, to cling on to every shred of Soviet earth and defend it to the utmost.

Our motherland is going through difficult days. At whatever the cost, we must stop and then throw back and destroy the enemy. The Germans are not as powerful as they seem to panickers. They are advancing with their last forces. Withstand their blows now, for the next few months, and this will mean the guarantee of our victory.

Can we absorb the attack and then throw the enemy back to the west? Yes we can, because our factories and enterprises in the rear are now working excellently and the front is receiving more and more planes, tanks, artillery and mortars.

What do we not have enough of?

We do not have sufficient order and discipline in companies, battalions, regiments, divisions, tank units and air squadrons. This is now our chief shortcoming. We must establish in our army strict order and iron discipline if we want to save the position and defend the motherland.

It is not permissible to tolerate any more commanders, commissars, political workers, units and formations who wilfully abandon military positions. It is not permissible to tolerate any more commanders. commissars, and political workers who allow panickers to determine the position on the field of battle and entice other soldiers to retreat and so open the front to the enemy.

Panickers and cowards must be eliminated on the spot.

Henceforth iron discipline is demanded of every commander, soldier and political worker – not a step back without orders from higher authorities.

Commanders of companies, battalions, regiments and divisions, and the responsible commissars and political workers retreating from military positions without orders from above are traitors to their country. Such officers and political workers will be treated as traitors of their country.

Such are the calls of our motherland.

To implement this order means the defence of our lands, the salvation of the motherland, and the extermination and destruction of a hateful enemy.

After its winter retreat before the vigorous pressure of the Red Army, when the discipline of the German forces began to crack, the Germans implemented severe measures to restore discipline, and with not bad results. They organised more than 100 penal companies for soldiers guilty of disciplinary offences of cowardice or wavering and placed them on the most dangerous sections of the front, ordering them to atone for their sins with their blood. They organised a further 10 or so penal battalions for officers guilty of disciplinary offences of cowardice or wavering, deprived them of their medals and placed them on even more dangerous sections of the front and ordered them to atone for their sins. Finally, they organised special blocking detachments, placed them behind wavering divisions and directed them to shoot panickers on the spot in the event of attempts at wilful abandonment of positions or attempts to surrender to captivity. As is well known, these actions had their effect and now the German forces fight better than they fought in winter. It turns out that the Germans have good discipline, although they have no noble aim of defending their motherland, only a predatory aim – to subjugate someone else's country – whereas our forces, having the noble aim of defending their desecrated country, do not have such discipline and therefore tolerate defeat.

Should one learn from the enemy in this matter, as in the past our ancestors learnt from the enemy and then went on to achieve victory?

I think that we ought to.

The Supreme Command of the Red Army orders:

1. Front Military Councils and, above all, Front Commanders:

    (a) to unconditionally liquidate the retreatist atmosphere among the troops and to cut with an iron hand propaganda that we could and should retreat further east, as if such a retreat would not be damaging;

(b) to unreservedly remove from post and send to head-quarters for court-martial Army Commanders per-mitting wilful retreat of troops from occupied positions without orders from the Front Commander;

(c) to organise on the front-line 1–3 (depending on the situation) penal battalions (of 800 people), to which will be sent middle-ranking and senior officers, and the corresponding political workers of all types of forces, guilty of disciplinary offences of cowardice or wavering, and to place them on the more difficult sections of the front in order that they have the possibility of atoning with blood for their crimes against the motherland.

2. Army Military Councils and, above all, Army Commanders:

(a) to unconditionally remove from posts commanders and commissars of corps and divisions permitting wilful retreat of troops from occupied positions with-out orders from Army Commanders and to send them to the Front Military Council for court-martial;

(b) to organise within the army 3–5 well-armed block-ing detachments (of up to 200 people each), place them in the immediate rear of wavering divisions, with the responsibility in the event of panic and disorderly retreat of the division's units, of executing on the spot panickers and cowards, thereby helping the honest soldiers of the division fulfil their duty to the motherland;

(c) to organise within the army 5–10 (depending on the situation) penal companies (of 150–200 people each), to which will be sent soldiers and junior offices guilty of disciplinary offences of cowardice or wavering and which will be placed in the most difficult sections of the army in order that they be given the chance to atone with their blood for their crimes against the motherland.

3. Commanders and Commissars of Corps and Divisions:

(a) to unreservedly remove from post commanders and commissars of regiments and battalions permitting wilful retreat of units without orders from Corps or Divisional Commanders, taking away their medals and decorations and sending them to the Front Military Council for court-martial;

(b) to render all assistance and support to the blocking detachments of the army strengthening order and discipline in units.

The order to be read in all companies, troops, squadrons, batteries, commands and staffs.

People's Commissar of Defence   *I. Stalin*

Translated from *Velikaya Otechestvennaya Voina, 1941–1945*,
Vol.1, Nauka: Moscow 1998, pp.503–7.

GLOSSARY OF MILITARY TERMS

Allies   The name given to the wartime coalition of America, Britain, the Soviet Union and other states. The Americans also used the term 'United Nations', while the Russians preferred 'Anti-Hitler' coalition or alliance. In the 1950s, Winston Churchill popularised use of the term 'Grand Alliance'.

Axis   The name given to the wartime alliance of Germany, Italy, Japan and other states. The term derives from a speech by Mussolini in November 1936 in which he spoke of the 'axis' of European politics now revolving around the German-Italian relationship.

Army   A military formation consisting of a variable number of corps (q.v.) and divisions (q.v.). A Soviet infantry army ranged from 50,000–100,000 strong, while Soviet tank armies were usually about half that size but with several hundred tanks and artillery pieces. German equivalents were substantially bigger, at least during the early years of the war.

Army Group   A military formation consisting of two or more armies (q.v.). The Soviet equivalents of Army Groups were Fronts (q.v.).

Blitzkrieg   German word meaning 'lightning war'.

Commissar   The Soviet equivalent of a government minister, but the term was also used for political officers attached to military units.

Corps   A military formation consisting of two or more divisions (q.v.). The Soviets also used the word corps to denote divisional (q.v.) strength tank and cavalry formations.

Division   A self-contained military formation consisting of a variable number of brigades, battalions and regiments and/or other sub-divisional units plus supporting specialist outfits. A full-strength German infantry division had 12,000–15,000 troops. A Panzer (q.v.) division was usually a bit bigger, with 100 or more tanks. Soviet divisions were in theory only slightly weaker than their German counterparts, but in practice were substantially weaker, often no more than a few thousand strong.

Eastern Front   The Soviet-German front during World War II (and World War I). However, from the Soviet point of view the Eastern Front was a Western Front. Alternative term: the Russian Front.

Front   Soviet equivalent of an Army Group (q.v.), often consisting of multiple armies with a total strength of 1–2 million troops.

GKO   Abbreviation of *Gosudarstvennyi Komitet Oborony*, the wartime State Defence Committee established in June 1941, headed by Stalin.

Guards   Title given to Soviet combat units that distinguished themselves in battle.

Marshal   The highest military rank in the German, Soviet and other armies.

OKH Abbreviation of *Oberkommando des Heeres* – High Command of the (German) Army. The OKH General Staff was headed by Franz Halder (1938–42) and Kurt Zeitzler (1942–4).

OKW Abbreviation of *Oberkommando der Wehrmacht* (q.v.) – High Command of the (German) Armed Forces. Effectively, Hitler's personal General Staff, with overall responsibility for army, airforce and navy strategy.

Panzer German word for a tank or armour.

Red Army The name of the Soviet army from January 1918, when the Workers and Peasants Red Army was formed. The name derived from armed units of workers in Petrograd in 1917 called 'Red Guards', red being the colour traditionally associated with left-wing revolutionaries since the French Revolution. The Red appellation was dropped after the Second World War.

Second Front Refers to the projected western Allied invasion of German-occupied Europe, the *first front* being the Eastern Front (q.v.). The Soviets began agitating for such an operation as early as summer 1941, but the western invasion of France (D-Day) did not take place until June 1944. However, public statements by the British and US governments in mid-1942 promising such an operation in the near future, convinced Hitler that an invasion was a serious, short-term prospect. This perception influenced the priority and urgency he attached to the Stalingrad campaign.

SS Abbreviation of *Schutzstaffel* (literally, protection squad). Originally, Hitler's personal security staff, the SS grew into a conglomerate economic, political, military and security organisation that was responsible for, among other things, the organisation and implementation of the Holocaust on the Eastern Front and then elsewhere in Europe.

Stavka   Russian word for headquarters. Used as shorthand for *Stavka Verkhovnogo Glavnokommandovaniya* – Headquarters of the Supreme Command.

Volgograd   The name of Stalingrad (formerly Tsaritsyn) since 1961.

Wehrmacht   The German armed forces (literally: defence power).

BIOGRAPHICAL NOTES

Chuikov, Vasilii Ivanovich (1900–82) Commander of the Soviet 62nd Army at Stalingrad. Led the 8th Guards Army (the re-named 62nd Army) to Berlin. Promoted to Marshal after the war. Deputy Commander and then Commander-in-Chief Soviet Occupation Forces in Germany, 1946–53. Commander, Kiev Military District, 1953–60. Deputy Minister of Defence and Commander-in-Chief, Soviet Ground Forces, 1960–5. From 1965 Chief of Civil Defence.

Ehrenburg, Il'ya Grigor'evich (1891–1967) Soviet writer and journalist. Prominent publicist and propagandist against fascism before the Second World War. During the war wrote for *Pravda*, *Izvestiya* and the Red Army newspaper, *Krasnaya Zvezda*. In the 1950s was a proponent of the liberalisation of Soviet culture and literature.

Grossman, Vasilii Semonovich (1905–64) Soviet writer and journalist. Special correspondent of Red Army newspaper, *Krasnaya Zvezda*, during the war. Later wrote fictionalised accounts of Stalingrad and the war, including, in the 1950s, the novel *Zhizn' i Sud'ba* (Life and Fate) which was not published in the Soviet Union until 1988.

Halder, Franz (1884–1972) Chief of the General Staff of the German Army (OKH) 1938–42. Resigned September 1942, following disagreements with Hitler (q.v.) over the Stalingrad campaign. After the July 1944 attempt on Hitler's life, although not a participant in the conspiracy, was imprisoned in Dachau concentration camp. Liberated by the

Americans in May 1945. After the war gave evidence against Nazi leaders at the Nuremberg trial.

Hitler, Adolf (1889–1945) Leader of the NSDAP (National Socialist German Workers Party, nicknamed the 'Nazis' by its opponents) from 1921. Appointed Chancellor of Germany, January 1933. Declared German '*Führer*' (Leader), August 1934. Became Commander-in-Chief of the German Armed Forces, December 1941. Committed suicide in Berlin on 30 April 1945.

Khrushchev, Nikita Sergeevich (1894–1971) Member of the Soviet politburo from 1939. Secretary of the Ukrainian Communist Party, 1938–47. The most senior political official present at the Front during the battle of Stalingrad. Became Soviet leader after Stalin's death in 1953. Ousted from power, 1964. Retired and wrote his memoirs.

Manstein, Eric von (1887–1973) Commander of the German 11th Army in the Crimea 1941–2. Promoted to Field Marshal in July 1942. Appointed Commander of Army Group Don in November 1942. Commander of unsuccessful German operation to rescue the 6th Army in Stalingrad in December 1942. From February 1943 commanded re-formed Army Group South. Relieved of his command March 1944. After the war, arrested and charged with war crimes. Sentenced to 18 years in 1950 but served only three.

Molotov, Vyacheslav Mikhailovich (1890–1986) Chairman of the Council of People's Commissars, 1930–1941. Soviet Foreign Minister 1939–9 and 1953–6. Best known for his association with the 'Molotov Cocktail' – a slang term for home-made petrol bombs – used at Stalingrad, and elsewhere. Origin of the term is disputed. Some say it dates from the Spanish Civil War and was used by anti-fascist Republicans because Molotov was Soviet premier at a time when the USSR was aiding Republican Spain in its struggle against Franco and the Fascists. Others argue that the term was first used, ironically and derogatorily, by Finns during the Winter War of 1939–40, when Molotov was Foreign Minister as well as Prime Minister and strongly identified with the Soviet attack on Finland.

Paulus, Fredrich Wilhelm Ernst (1890–1957). Chief-of-Staff of the 6th Army, 1939–40. September 1940 appointed Deputy Chief of Staff of the German Army under General Franz Halder (q.v.). Played a leading role in planning Operation Barbarossa. Appointed Commander of the 6th Army in January 1942, in succession to Field Marshal Walter von Reichenau, who had been appointed to command Army Group South in December 1941 (but who died in an air crash in January 1942). Promoted to Colonel-General in November 1942 and to Field Marshal in January 1943. Captured at Stalingrad on 31 January 1943. Gave evidence at the Nuremberg trial of Nazi leaders in 1946. Released from Soviet captivity in 1953 and retired to Dresden in communist East Germany.

Rodimtsev, Aleksandr Il'ich (1905–77) Commander of the Soviet 13th Guards Division at Stalingrad. Subsequently commanded 32nd Guards Corps and took part in the liberation of Poland and the Ukraine and in the assault on Germany and Berlin.

Seydlitz-Kurzbach, Walther von (1888–1976) Commander of German 51st Corps during the battle of Stalingrad. Captured at Stalingrad, and in 1943 emerged as a leading figure in the Soviet-sponsored League of German Officers and the National Committee for a Free Germany. Charged with war crimes by the Russians in 1950 and sentenced to 25 years. Released and repatriated to West Germany in 1955.

Simonov, Konstantin Mikhailovich (1915–1979) Soviet poet, dramatist, novelist and journalist. During World War II was special correspondent of the Red Army newspaper, *Krasnaya Zvezda*. After the war wrote numerous fictionalised and memoir accounts of his and others' experiences during Great Patriotic War.

Stalin, Joseph Vissarionovich (1879–1953) General-Secretary of the Soviet Communist Party, 1922–53. Became Chairman of the Council of People's Commissars, May 1941. After the outbreak of war on 22 June 1941, became Chairman of the State Committee of Defence (30 June); head of the *Stavka* of the Supreme Command (10 July); People's Commissar for Defence (19 July); and Supreme Commander of the Armed Forces (8 August). In June 1945 given the title of *Generalissimo* (i.e. the supreme General).

Vasilevskii, Alexander Mikhailovich (1895–1977) Deputy Chief of the Soviet General Staff and Chief of Operations, 1941–2. Appointed Chief of the General Staff, June 1942. Promoted to Marshal, February 1943. From February 1945, Commander of the 3rd Belorussian Front. Appointed Supreme Commander of Soviet Forces in the Far East, June 1945. Chief of the General Staff and First Deputy Minister of the Armed Forces, 1946–9. Minister of the Armed Forces, 1949–53. First Deputy Minister of Defence, 1953–7. Retired, December 1957.

Zeitzler, Kurt (1895–1963) Appointed Chief of the General Staff of the German Army in September 1942, in succession to Halder (q.v.). Served in post until July 1944. In the 1950s wrote an early German account of the battle of Stalingrad.

Zhukov, Georgii Konstantinovich (1896–1974) Chief of the Soviet General Staff, 1941. Commander, Western Front, 1942. Appointed Deputy Supreme Commander and Deputy People's Commissar of Defence, August 1942. Promoted to Marshal, January 1943. Commander, 1st Ukrainian Front, 1944 and 1st Belorussian Front, 1945. Commander in Chief, Soviet occupation forces in Germany, 1945–6. Commander, Odessa, then Ural Military District, 1947–52. First Deputy Minister of Defence, 1953–5. Minister of Defence 1955–7. Fell out with Khrushchev (q.v.) and removed from all party and state offices, October 1957. Returned to grace, mid-1960s, after Khrushchev's fall from power.

ADDITIONAL SOURCES

Kto Byl Kto v Velikoi Otechestvennoi Voine, 1941–1945 (Moscow, 2000).

Richard Holmes (ed.), *The Oxford Companion to Military History* (Oxford, 2001).

Warren Shaw and David Pryce, *Encyclopedia of the USSR* (London, 1990).

Christopher Tunney, *A Biographical Dictionary of World War II* (London, 1972).

GUIDE TO FURTHER READING

1. THE SOVIET-GERMAN WAR

Forty years ago William L. Shirer said of Alexander Werth's *Russia at War, 1941–1945* (Barrie & Rockcliff: London 1964; reissued by Pan Books: London 1965) that it was 'the best book we probably shall ever have in English about Russia at war'. Amazingly, it is an assessment that remains true. No other book matches Werth's magnificent combination of military narrative, political and social analysis, and participant-observation. Werth was the Moscow correspondent of *The Sunday Times* during the war, and his brilliantly written account really does tell it like it actually was. The book incorporates material from two earlier works by Werth: *Moscow '41* (Hamish Hamilton: London 1942), a diary of his first year in wartime Moscow, and *The Year of Stalingrad* (Hamish Hamilton: London 1946). The latter text, the first substantial postwar account of the battle, incorporates a wealth of contemporary material from the press and other Soviet sources.

Contemporary readers are also fortunate to have at their disposal two other outstanding general accounts of the Soviet war with Germany: David M. Glantz & Jonathan House, *When Titans Clashed: How the Red Army Stopped Hitler* (University Press of Kansas: Lawrence, Kansas 1995) and Richard Overy, *Russia's War* (Allen Lane: London 1997). Overy also deals with various aspects of the Soviet-German War in his *Why the Allies Won* (Jonathan Cape: London 1995), which includes an excellent summary chapter on

'Deep War: Stalingrad and Kursk'. For an official Soviet overview of the war see *Great Patriotic War of the Soviet Union, 1941–1945* (Progress Publishers: Moscow 1974). A history of the conflict that tells the story from the point of view of Soviet participants is Albert Axell, *Russia's Heroes, 1941–1945* (Constable: London 2001).

Books which deal with the Eastern Front more from the German perspective include two older works, which are still of great value and interest: Alan Clark, *Barbarossa: The Russian-German Conflict, 1941–1945* (Weidenfeld & Nicolson: London 1965, reissued 1995) and Albert Seaton, *The Russo-German War, 1941–45* (Arthur Barker: London 1971). A popular account of the war by a German author is Paul Carrell's multi-volume *Hitler's War on Russia* (George Harrap: London 1964, reissued 1970–71).

The standard operational histories of the war are John Erickson's two volumes on 'Stalin's War with Germany': *The Road to Stalingrad* (Harper & Row: New York 1975) and *The Road to Berlin* (Weidenfeld and Nicolson: London 1983); and Earl F. Ziemke's *Moscow to Stalingrad: Decision in the East* (co-author Magna E. Bauer, Center of Military History, United States Army: Washington D.C. 1987) and *From Stalingrad to Berlin: The German Defeat in the East* (Center of Military History, United States Army: Washington D.C. 1968). I have referred extensively to these indispensable texts in my own account.

The earliest postwar effort at an overall narrative of the Eastern Front war was General Augustin Guillaume, *La*

Guerre Germano-Soviétique, 1941–1945 (Paris 1949, published in English by the British War Office as *The German Russian War, 1941–1945* (The War Office: London 1956).

For an understanding of the historical context of what happened during the war, I would recommend, on the Soviet side: Geoffrey Hosking, *A History of the Soviet Union* (Fontana Press: London 1990); Robert Service, *A History of Twentieth-Century Russia* (Penguin: London 1997); and Michel Heller and Aleksandr Nekrich, *Utopia in Power* (Hutchinson: London 1986). All have excellent chapters on the Great Patriotic War. For the German side, I recommend the second volume of Ian Kershaw's *Hitler* (Penguin: London 2000) and Alan Bullock, *Hitler and Stalin: Parallel Lives* (HarperCollins: London 1991).

2. THE BATTLE OF STALINGRAD

The two great popular accounts of the battle are William Craig, *Enemy at the Gates: The Battle for Stalingrad* (Hodder and Stoughton: London 1973, reissued 2001) and Antony Beevor, *Stalingrad* (Penguin: London 1999). Both are very good value as micro-level accounts of the battle from the point of view of participants. But I found the clearest account of the course of the battle in the city to be Stephen Walsh, *Stalingrad, 1942–1943: The Infernal Cauldron* (Simon & Schuster: London 2000). Written by a Sandhurst Military Academy historian, the book is also strong on relevant aspects of military doctrine and quite up to date on the new view of the battle emerging from research on Soviet sources by David Glantz and others. It is a large-scale format production and contains some great photographs. Another exceptionally clear, short account, which I also found very useful, is Geoffrey Jukes, *Stalingrad: The Turning Point* (Ballatine Books: New York 1968). Also of interest and value are Ronald Seth, *Stalingrad – Point of Return* (Victor Gollancz: London 1959), V.E. Tarrant, *Stalingrad: Anatomy of an Agony* (Leo Cooper: London 1992) and Edwin P. Hoyt, *199 Days: The Battle for Stalingrad* (Forge: New York 1993). Walter Kerr, *The Secret of Stalingrad* (Doubleday: New York 1978) makes use of a lot of published Soviet material. During the war Kerr was Moscow correspondent of the New York Herald-Tribune and published *The Russian Army: Its Men, Its Leaders and Its Battles* (Alfred A. Knopf: New York 1944). Another wartime text which, naturally, focuses on Stalingrad is W.E.D. Allen and Paul Muratoff, *The Russian Campaigns of 1941–43* (Penguin: London 1944).

An early German account of the battle, first published in 1953, was Heinz Schröter, *Stalingrad* (Michael Joseph: London 1958). Schroter was a war correspondent and his account apparently started life as a wartime study prepared for Goebbel's Propaganda Ministry, which then decided not to publish it. The book illustrates a common postwar German theme of Stalingrad as unnecessary human folly, tragedy and sacrifice. Another example in the same genre is Paul Carell, *Stalingrad: The Defeat of the German 6th Army* (Schiffer Publishers: Atglen, PA 1993).

To convey the flavour of the battle I relied a lot on contemporary Soviet reportage. One of the key collections is *Stalingrad* (Foreign Languages Publishing House: Moscow

1943). Fictionalised Soviet accounts of Stalingrad included Konstantin Simonov *Days and Nights* (Simon and Schuster: New York 1945); Victor Nekrasov, *Front-Line Stalingrad* (Harvill Press: London 1962), written by a soldier-participant in the battle; and Vasilii Grossman, *Life and Fate* (Harper and Row: New York 1986). A collection of wartime articles by Ilya Ehrenburg and Simonov was published in *In One Newspaper*, (Sphinx Press: New York 1985). Interestingly, the collection did not include the two authors' anti-German hate propaganda. Fictional German equivalents include Heinrich Gerlach, *The Forsaken Army* (Weidenfeld and Nicholson: London 1958) and Heinz Konsalik, *The Heart of the 6th Army* (W.H. Allen: London 1977). David L. Robbins, *War of the Rats* (Bantam Books 1999) is a novel by an American author based on the contest between German and Soviet snipers in Stalingrad.

On the Stalingrad campaign as a whole there is nothing better than the detailed, careful and balanced research of Bernd Wegner, 'The War Against the Soviet Union, 1942–1943' in volume 6 of the collective work H. Boog et al, *Germany and the Second World War* (Clarendon Press: Oxford 2001). Wegner has also published a valuable summary article: 'The Road to Defeat: The German Campaigns in Russia 1941–43' (*The Journal of Strategic Studies*, no.1, vol.13, March 1990).

The very first operational history of the battle, and still useful, was the 1943 Soviet General Staff Study, later edited and published by Louis C. Rotundo, *Battle for Stalingrad: The 1943 Soviet General Staff Study* (Pergagamon-Brassey's: London 1989).

3. MEMOIRS

We are fortunate to have available in English most of the important German and Soviet military memoirs of Stalingrad.

Leading the charge on the Soviet side was General Vasilii Chuikov's memorable account of the Stalingrad city battle, *The Beginning of the Road* (MacGibbon and Kee: London 1963). There are various versions of Marshal Georgii Zhukov's memoirs. In English the best bet is the two-volume G. Zhukov, *Reminiscences and Reflections* (Progress Publishers: Moscow 1985). There is also Georgii K. Zhukov, *Marshal Zhukov's Greatest Battles* (MacDonald: London 1969) which contains translations of articles by Zhukov on the battles of Moscow, Stalingrad, Kursk and Berlin first published in *Voenno-Istoricheskii Zhurnal* (Military-History Journal) in the 1960s. (The best Russian edition of Zhukov's memoirs is the 10th, published in Moscow in 1990, but treatment of Stalingrad does not vary much in the different versions published since the 1960s). Marshal Alexander M. Vasilevskii's account of the war may be found in *A Lifelong Cause* (Progress Publishers: Moscow 1973). Marshal Konstantin Rokossovsky's *A Soldier's Duty* (Progress Publishers: Moscow 1970) deals, in particular, with the counteroffensive at Stalingrad. There are two good collections of Soviet military memoirs: Seweryn Bialer (ed), *Stalin and His Generals: Soviet Military Memoirs of World War II* (Souvenir Press: London 1969) and *Two Hundred Days of Fire: Accounts by Participants and Witnesses of the Battle of Stalingrad* (Progress Publishers: Moscow 1970). The latter, an official

Soviet collection, contains contributions by N.N. Voronov, the artillery chief, A.I. Yeremenko, the Stalingrad Front commander, S.I. Rudenko, the air marshal and A.I. Rodimtsev, the commander of the heroic 13th Guards Division. There is also Andrei Grechko, *Battle for the Caucasus* (Progress Publishers: Moscow 1971). Interesting from the point of view of post-communist Soviet military memoirs is Albert Axell, *Stalin's War Through the Eyes of His Commanders* (Arms and Armour Press: London 1997). A unique overview of the workings of the Soviet General Staff during the war is provided by the Chief of Operations and Deputy Chief, S.M. Shtemenko, *The Soviet General Staff at War, 1941–1945* (two vols., Progress Publishers: Moscow 1970, 1986). For guidance on 'reading' these memoirs consult the studies in Harold Shukman (ed), *Stalin's Generals* (Grove Press: New York 1993) and Albert Seaton, *Stalin as Warlord* (Batsford: London 1976). The only major biography in English of a Soviet wartime General is Otto Preston Chaney, *Zhukov* (rev.ed., University of Oklahoma Press: London 1996).

The one important command-level Soviet memoir that remains untranslated (although it is available in French and German) is Marshal A.I. Yeremenko's *Stalingrad* (Voenno Izdatel'stvo Ministerstva Oborony Souza SSSR: Moscow 1961). Yeremenko was commander of the Stalingrad Front in 1942–43, which at the time of the city battle included Chuikov's 62nd Army in its remit. Yeremenko's memoirs are controversial because of the emphasis placed on his and Khrushchev's role in winning the battle (they were published when the latter was Soviet leader). In 1961 Yeremenko told

Dennis Ogden, the *Daily Worker* correspondent in Moscow, that the only problem with the battle of Stalingrad was that it should never have taken place there, meaning that this decisive encounter should have been fought hundreds of miles to the west – an off-the-record remark which pointed up Stalin's responsibility for misreading the intelligence on the German 'surprise' attack of June 1941.

Nikita Khrushchev was chief Soviet political commissar during the Stalingrad campaign and battle. For his account of events see *Khrushchev Remembers* (two vols., Andre Deutsch: London 1971, 1974).

On the German side a good place to start is B.H. Liddell Hart, *The German Generals Talk* (William Morrow: New York 1948) – interviews conducted by the author not long after the war, when many of the top German commanders were still imprisoned by the western allies. Then there is Franz Halder, *Hitler as War Lord* (Putnam: London 1950) and *The Halder Diaries* (Westview Press: Boulder, Colo. 1976); Erich von Manstein, *Lost Victories* (Methuen: London 1959); Walter Warlimont, *Inside Hitler's Headquarters* (Frederick A. Praeger: New York 1964); and Kurt Zeitzler, 'Stalingrad' in William Richardson and Seymour Freidin (eds), *The Fatal Decisions* (Michael Joseph: London 1956). Paulus's memoirs are available in the form of his notes, correspondence and documents, which are the basis of Walter Göerlitz, *Paulus and Stalingrad* (Methuen: London 1963). Published only in German is General Walther von Seydlitz's account *Stalingrad: Konflikt und Konsequenz* (Stalling: Oldenburg 1977).

4. SPECIALIST STUDIES

On the origins of the Soviet-German War I would recommend the various studies in volume four of H. Boog et al, *Germany and the Second World War (The Attack on the Soviet Union)* (Clarendon Press: Oxford 1998) and G. Gorodetsky, *Grand Delusion: Stalin and the German Invasion of Russia* (Yale University Press: London 1999). I have also made a modest contribution to this topic myself in various writings, including *The Soviet Union and the Origins of the Second World War: Russo-German Relations and the Road to War, 1933–1941* (Macmillan: London 1995).

The western guru of Soviet military history during World War II is David M. Glantz, who has published innumerable books on the topic. The ones I found most useful for this book were: *Soviet Military Deception in the Second World War* (Frank Cass: London 1989); *Barbarossa: Hitler's Invasion of Russia 1941* (Tempus: Stroud 2001); *Kharkov 1942: Anatomy of a Military Disaster Through Soviet Eyes* (Ian Allan: Shepperton 1998); *Zhukov's Greatest Defeat: The Red Army's Epic Disaster in Operation Mars, 1942* (Ian Allan: Shepperton 2000); and (with Jonathan M. House) *The Battle of Kursk* (University Press of Kansas: Lawrence 1999).

An important and innovative study of the German side of Stalingrad is Joel S.A. Hayward, *Stopped at Stalingrad: The Luftwaffe and Hitler's Defeat in the East, 1942–1943* (University Press of Kansas: Lawrence 1998). Hayward is also the author of 'Hitler's Quest for Oil: the Impact of Economic Considerations on Military Strategy, 1941–1942'

(*The Journal of Strategic Studies*, no.4, vol.18, December 1995).

An important study of German decision-making during the Stalingrad campaign is Geoffrey Jukes, *Hitler's Stalingrad Decisions* (University of California Press: Berkeley 1985). The book also contains a useful chapter comparing Hitler and Stalin's roles during the campaign. Jukes' text may be usefully supplemented by firsthand acquaintance with Hitler's war directives in H.R. Trevor-Roper, *Hitler's War Directives, 1939–1945* (Sidgwick and Jackson: London 1964).

On Germany's war of annihilation in the east I have relied mainly on Omer Bartov, Jürgen Förster and Christian Streit. Their views are summarised in essays published in David Cesarani (ed), *The Final Solution: Origins and Implementation* (Routledge: London 1994). There is also the important collection Hannes Heere & Klaus Naumann (eds), *War of Extermination: The German Military in World War II, 1941-1944* (Berghahn Books: New York 1999) and Omer Bartov, *The Eastern Front, 1941–45, German Troops and the Barbarisation of Warfare* (Palgrave: London 1985, reissued 2001). On the massacre of Soviet Jewry, see Lucjan Dbroszycki & Jeffrey S. Gurock (eds), *The Holocaust in the Soviet Union* (M.E. Sharpe: New York 1993). For an alternative view, which emphasises the Soviet contribution to the annihilatory character of the war on the Eastern Front, see Joachim Hoffmann's contribution to Boog et al (1998). Far more tendentious, controversial and extreme is Hoffmann's book *Stalin's War of Extermination, 1941–1945* (Theses & Dissertations Press: Capshaw 2001). Compare, for example, what Hoffman says (chap.3) about orders 270 and 227 with the actual texts, which are published in this volume.

On the Red Army's assault on Germany in 1945 there is Cornelius Ryan, *The Last Battle* (Collins: London 1966); Christopher Duffy, *Red Storm on the Reich: The Soviet March on Germany, 1945* (Routledge: London 1991); Anthony Read and David Fisher, *The Fall of Berlin* (Pimlico 1993, 2002); and Antony Beevor, *Berlin: The Downfall 1945* (Penguin: London 2002). On the Red Army rapes controversy there is an outstanding chapter in Norman M. Naimark, *The Russians in Germany: A History of the Soviet Zone of Occupation, 1945–1949* (Harvard University Press: Cambridge, Mass. 1995). Some context for Soviet retribution and revenge may be found in Istvan Deak et al, *The Politics of Retribution in Europe: World War II and Its Aftermath* (Princeton University Press: Princeton 2000).

On the Soviet economy during the war the most important work is that by Mark Harrison, particularly *Soviet Planning in Peace and War, 1938–1945* (Cambridge University Press: Cambridge 1988) and *Accounting for War: Soviet Production, Employment and the Defence Burden, 1940–1945* (Cambridge University Press: Cambridge 1996). Harrison is also the co-author with John Barber of the standard text on the social history of the Soviet Union during World War II: *The Soviet Home Front, 1941–1945* (Longman: London 1991). Four other highly illuminating texts on related topics are Susan J. Linz (ed), *The Impact of World War II on the Soviet Union* (Rowman & Allanheld: Totowa, NJ: 1985); John & Carol Garrard (eds). *World War 2 and the Soviet People* (St Martin's

Press: New York 1993); Richard Stites (ed), *Culture and Entertainment in Wartime Russia* (Indiana University Press: Bloomington 1995); and Robert E. Thurston and Bernd Bonwetsch (eds), *The People's War: Responses to World War II in the Soviet Union* (University of Illinois Press: Urbana 2000).

For some illuminating comparisons between Soviet Russia and Nazi Germany, including during World War II, see Ian Kershaw and Moshe Lewin, *Stalinism and Nazism* (Cambridge University Press: Cambridge 1997).

On historiographical issues there is R.J.B. Bosworth, *Explaining Auschwitz & Hiroshima: History Writing and the Second World War, 1945–1990* (Routledge: London 1993); Matthew P. Gallagher, *The Soviet History of World War II: Myths, Memoirs and Realities* (Frederick A. Praeger: New York 1963); Charles S. Maier, *The Unmasterable Past: History, Holocaust and German National Identity* (Harvard University Press: Cambridge, Mass. 1998); and Robert G. Moeller, *War Stories: The Search for a Usable Past in the Federal Republic of Germany* (University of California Press: Berkeley 2001).

P.M.H. Bell, *John Bull and the Bear: British Public Opinion, Foreign Policy and the Soviet Union 1941–1945* (Edward Arnold: London 1990) is very interesting on the British popular response to Stalingrad. Alan J. Levine puts the argument that Stalingrad didn't matter much anyway in 'Was World War II a Near-Run Thing?' (*The Journal of Strategic Studies*, no.1, vol.8, January 1985).

5. WORKS IN GERMAN AND RUSSIAN

English-language books on Stalingrad are quite extensive, but nothing compared to the massive body of work published in German and Russian. The indispensable bibliographic guide to this work is Rolf-Dieter Müller & Gerd R. Ueberschär (eds), *Hitler's War in the East, 1941–1945: A Critical Assessment* (Berghahn Books: Oxford 1997), which informs us that there are over 200 publications dealing with the battle of Stalingrad alone, most of them in German or Russian. As well as listing books and articles, the two editors provide an invaluable summary of the main lines of research and argument in a broad range of literature on the German-Soviet war.

Muller and Ueberschar can be usefully supplemented by reference by the massive annotated bibliography of Michael Parrish, *The USSR in World War II* (two vols., Garland Publishers: New York 1981). The bibliographies of Erickson (1975 and 1983) and Bauer and Ziemke (1987) are also usefully annotated. Finally, there is Joachim Wieder's discussion of the Stalingrad literature in his *Stalingrad: Memories and Reassessments* (Arms and Armour: London 1995), but readers may find the style of the English translation somewhat difficult to follow.

The key German works on the Stalingrad campaign are Hans Doerr, *Der Feldzug nach Stalingrad* (E.S. Mittler & Sohn: Darmstadt 1955, the first professional German study, which was also published in Russian translation in 1957); Manfred Kehrig, *Stalingrad* (Deutsche Verlags-Anstalt: Stuttgart 1974, which contains a number of important documents, but only covers the battle from November 1942 onwards); and the Bernd Wegner study noted above, which is now available in English. Another important strand of German research has been on the myths and legends of Stalingrad. See Jens Ebert (ed), *Stalingrad – eine deutsche Legende* (Rowohlt: Hamburg 1992) and Wolfram Wette and Gerd R. Ueberschär (eds), *Stalingrad: Mythos und Wirklichkeit einer Schlacht* (Fischer Taschenbuch Verlag: Frankfurt 1992). An important work on the political and military consequences of Stalingrad for the Axis alliance is Jürgen Förster, *Stalingrad: Risse in Bündis, 1942/43* (Verlag Rombach Freiburg: Freiburg 1975). Förster also edited *Stalingrad: Ereignis-Wirkung-Symbol* (Piper: Munich 1992). This was an international symposium, with American, British and Russian contributors, as well as German. The volume was also published in Russian: *Stalingrad: Sobytiye, Vozdeistviye, Simbol* (Progress-Akademiya: Moscow 1995).

In Russian the key text is Alexander M. Samsonov's detailed study *Stalingradskaya Bitva* (Nauka: Moscow 1960, 1968, 1983, 1989). Another foundational text of the Soviet historiography of Stalingrad is Marshal Konstantin K. Rokossovsky (ed), *Velikaya Pobeda na Volge* (Voenizdat: Moscow 1965). A large and important collection of memoirs was published in *Stalingradskaya Epopeya* (Nauka: Moscow 1968). A unique account is Aleksei S. Chuyanov, *Stalingradskii Dnevnik (1941–1943)* (Volgograd 1979) – the diary of the leader of the Stalingrad Communist Party.

In 'official' Soviet histories Stalingrad is treated in *Istoriya*

Velikoi Otechestvennoi Voiny Sovetskogo Souza, 1941–1945, vol.3 (Institut Marksizma-Leninizma: Moscow 1963, the Khrushchevite treatment); *Istoriya Vtoroi Mirovoi Voiny, 1939–1945*, vols 5–6 (Voenizdat: Moscow 1975 and 1976, the Brezhnevite version); and *Velikaya Otechestvennaya Voina, 1941–1945*, vols 1–2 (Nauka: Moscow 1998, the post-Soviet account). A collection illustrating the development of a more critical discussion of Stalingrad in post-Communist Russia is B.S. Abalikhina (ed), *Stalingradskaya Bitva* (Volgograd 1994).

REFERENCES

Albert Axell, *Russia's Heroes, 1941–1945* (Constable: London 2001)

John Barber & Mark Harrison, *The Soviet Home Front, 1941–1945* (Longman: London 1991)

Omer Bartov, *The Eastern Front, 1941–1945, German Troops and the Barbarisation of Warfare* (Palgrave: London, 1985, 2001)

Antony Beevor, *Stalingrad* (Penguin: London 1999)

Antony Beevor, *Berlin: The Downfall 1945* (Penguin: London 2002)

Günter Bischof, *Austria in the First Cold War, 1945–55* (Macmillan: London 1999)

Horst Boog et al, *Germany and the Second World War*, vol.4 (Clarendon Press: Oxford 1998)

Horst Boog et al, *Germany and the Second World War*, vol.6 (Clarendon Press: Oxford 2001)

David Cesarani (ed), *The Final Solution* (Routledge: London 1994)

Vasilii Chuikov, *The Beginning of the Road* (MacGibbon and Kee: London 1963)

Winston S. Churchill, *The Second World War*, vol.4 (Cassell: London 1951)

Alan Clark, *Barbarossa: The Russian–German Conflict, 1941–1945* (Weidenfeld & Nicolson: London 1965)

R.W. Davies, *Soviet History in the Gorbachev Revolution* (Macmillan: London 1989)

Christopher Duffy, *Red Storm on the Reich: The Soviet March on Germany, 1945* (Routledge: London 1991)

John Erickson, *The Road to Stalingrad* (Harper & Row: New York 1975)

John Erickson, *The Road to Berlin* (Weidenfeld & Nicolson: London 1983)

David M. Glantz, *Soviet Military Deception in the Second World War* (Frank Cass: London 1989)

David M. Glantz, *Zhukov's Greatest Defeat* (Ian Allan: Shepperton 2000)

David M. Glantz, *Barbarossa* (Tempus: Stroud 2001)

David M. Glantz & Jonathan House, *When Titans Clashed: How the Red Army Stopped Hitler* (University Press of Kansas: Lawrence, Kansas 1995)

Walter Göerlitz, *Paulus and Stalingrad* (Methuen: London 1963)

Mark Harrison, *Soviet Planning in Peace and War, 1938–1945* (Cambridge University Press: Cambridge 1988)

Mark Harrison, 'The USSR and Total War: Why Didn't the Soviet Economy Collapse in 1942?' in Roger Chickering and Stig Forster (eds), *A World in Total War* (Cambridge University Press: Cambridge 2002)

Joel S.A. Hayward, *Stopped at Stalingrad: The Luftwaffe and*

Hitler's Defeat in the East, 1942–1943 (University of Kansas Press: Lawrence, Kansas 1998)

Hannes Heere & Klaus Naumann (eds), *War of Extermination: The German Military in World War II* (Berghahn Books: New York 1999)

Michel Heller & Alexksandr Nekrich, *Utopia in Power* (Hutchinson: London 1986)

Geoffrey Hosking, *A History of the Soviet Union* (Fontana Press: London 1990)

Geoffrey Jukes, *Stalingrad: The Turning Point* (Ballantine Books: New York 1968)

Geoffrey Jukes, *Hitler's Stalingrad Decisions* (University of California Press: Berkeley 1985)

Manfred Kehrig, *Stalingrad* (Deutsche Verlags-Anstalt: Stuttgart 1974)

Mark Kramer, 'The Soviet Union and the Founding of the German Democratic Republic', Europe-Asia Studies, vol.51, no.6, 1999

Alan J. Levine, 'Was World War II a Near-Run Thing?', The Journal of Strategic Studies, no.1, vol.8, January 1985

B.H. Liddell Hart, *The German Generals Talk* (William Morrow: New York 1948)

Henri Michel, *The Second World War*, vol.1 (Praeger Publishers: New York 1975)

Robert G. Moeller, *War Stories: The Search for a Usable Past in the Federal Republic of Germany* (University of California Press: Berkeley 2001)

Rolf-Dieter Müller & Gerd R. Ueberschar (eds), *Hitler's War in the East, 1941–1945: A Critical Assessment* (Berghahn Books: Oxford 1997)

Norman M. Naimark, *The Russians in Germany: A History of*

the Soviet Zone of Occupation, 1945–1949 (Harvard University Press: Cambridge, Mass. 1995)

Jeremy Noakes & Geoffrey Pridham, *Nazism 1919–1945*, vol.3 (University of Exeter Press: Exeter 1988)

Richard Overy, *Why the Allies Won* (Jonathan Cape: London 1995)

Richard Overy, *Russia's War* (Allen Lane: London 1997)

Richard Overy, *The Battle* (Penguin: London 2000)

Anthony Read and David Fisher, *The Fall of Berlin* (Pimlico: London 1993, 2002)

Alexander M. Samsonov, *Stalingradskaya Bitva* (Nauka: Moscow 1968)

Albert Seaton, *The Russo-German War, 1941–45* (Arthur Barker: London 1971)

Elena S. Senyavskaya, *Psikhologia Voiny v XX Veke: Istoricheskii Opyt Rossii* (Rosspen: Moscow 1999)

Robert Service, *A History of Twentieth-Century Russia* (Penguin: London 1997)

Stalingrad (Foreign Languages Publishing House: Moscow 1943)

J.V. Stalin, *On the Great Patriotic War of the Soviet Union* (Hutchinson: London 1943)

V.E. Tarrant, *Stalingrad: Anatomy of an Agony* (Leo Cooper: London 1992)

H.R. Trevor-Roper, *Hitler's War Directives, 1939–1945* (Sidgwick and Jackson: London 1964)

Two Hundred Days of Fire: Accounts by Participants and Witnesses of the Battle of Stalingrad (Progress Publishers: Moscow 1970)

Stephen Walsh, *Stalingrad, 1942–1943: The Infernal Cauldron* (Simon & Schuster: London 2000)

Alexander Werth, *The Year of Stalingrad* (Hamish Hamilton: London 1946)

Alexander Werth, *Russia at War* (Barrie and Rockcliff: London 1964)

Yevgeny Yevtushenko, *Selected Poems* (Penguin: London 1962)

Kurt Zeitzler, 'Stalingrad' in William Richardson and Seymour Freidin (eds), *The Fatal Decisions* (Michael Joseph: London 1956)

Georgii Zhukov, *Reminiscences and Reflections*, vol.2 (Progress Publishers: Moscow 1985)

Earl F. Ziemke & Magna E. Bauer, *Moscow to Stalingrad: Decision in the East* (Center of Military History, United States Army: Washington DC 1987)

INDEX